French Revolution
FOR BEGINNERS

UNITÉ
INDIVISIBILITÉ
NITÉ
EGALITÉ

D0776481

Martin McCrory
& Robert Moulder

Writers and Readers

Writers and Readers Publishing Cooperative Society Ltd
144 Camden High Street, London NW1 0NE
England

Published by Writers and Readers Publishing Cooperative Ltd
Text Copyright © 1983 Martin McCrory
Illustrations Copyright © 1983 Robert Moulder
Hand Lettering by Jim Fortey

All Rights Reserved

Series Editor: Richard Appignanesi
Cover Design: Louise Fili
Set in Helvetica
Typeset by Rowland Phototypesetting (London) Limited
Printed in Great Britain at the University Press, Oxford

ISBN Case 0 86316 014 X
ISBN Paper 0 86316 015 8

FRANCE IN 1789

0 50 100 150 K

Chapter one

THE ANCIEN REGIME

THE COURT OF LOUIS XIV

The late seventeenth-century saw the emergence of France as one of the most influential powers in the European world. The violent power struggles of the French nobility were reduced to an undignified squabble over points of etiquette as the theory and practice of royal absolutism came together in the person of Louis XIV, the 'Sun King'.

The magnificent palace of Versailles was the outward expression of Louis' autocratic rule, designed to convey the grandeur and authority of the Bourbon monarchy. To the guests at the elaborate banquets held in the Hall of Mirrors it would have seemed inconceivable that within two generations after Louis' death in 1715, France would be plunged into a turmoil of social and political chaos culminating in the violent destruction of the Ancien Régime.

greatness in size

impossible

to the highest point

France in the eighteenth century

The accession of Louis XVI in 1774 was an unfortunate event for a nation in crisis. Duller than either of his brothers, he was to display scant interest or aptitude in affairs of state. At a time when France required a strong monarch, Louis' lack of character was to make him dangerously vunerable to pressure from an aristocracy desperate for control of state machinery. Fatally indecisive, the events of 1789 were to take him by surprise, while his apparent inability either to understand or accept them was to have a profound effect on the increasingly violent escalation of the Revolution.

THE ROYAL CLIQUE
1. LOUIS XVI, 2. COMTE DE PROVENCE, THE KING'S BROTHER, 3. COMTESSE DE POLIGNAC, INTIMATE FRIEND OF THE QUEEN, 4. COMTE D'ARTOIS KING'S YOUNGEST BROTHER, 5. AXEL DE FERSEN SWEDISH NOBLEMAN, REPUTED LOVER OF THE QUEEN, 6. QUEEN MARIE ANTOINETTE WITH THE ROYAL CHILDREN

The wars of the eighteenth-century had left France financially depleted with the high cost of maintaining a standing army, a disastrous drain on available resources. The Seven Years War (1756-63) in particular dealt a bitter blow to any hope of recovery, resulting as it did in the virtual destruction of France's lucrative colonial empire.

The American War of Independence gave a much-needed boost to French prestige, but at the cost of an alarming increase in state expenditure. Entering into an alliance with the United States after the battle of Saratoga (October 1777), France supplied the rebels with arms, ammunition and an expeditionary force of 8,000 men under the command of Rochambeau. To finance this involvement, the French government was forced to make loans at ruinous interest rates of 8 – 10%. This massive investment in American freedom was to bring France little save near-bankruptcy and a growing interest in the principles of liberty and equality.

THE SOCIAL CLASSES

Eighteenth Century French society consisted of a bewildering hierarchy of Social Categories and legally classified Orders. Within this complicated structure, it is however possible to distinguish 4 main groupings.

Nobility

The nobility comprised only 1.5% of the total population. Prior to 1750, entry had been relatively easy, with venality of office creating a 'nobility of the robe' alongside the hereditary nobles. In the later 18th Century, the nobility began to close their ranks, reserving principle positions in the state, church and armed forces for themselves.

Bourgeoisie

Divided between wealthy landowners (an intermediary class between bourgeois and noble referred to as 'notables') and highly-placed civil servants and financiers. Their common aspiration was to enter the ranks of the nobility. Exasperation at the unavailability of state posts made them willing to entertain a tacit alliance with the lower classes against those nobles who stood in their way.

Petit bourgeoisie

Disdainfully referred to by the upper bourgeoisie as 'the people', they included members of the professions, artisans and tradesmen, all ranked according to their prosperity. Resentful of the arrogant upper bourgeoisie, they in turn regarded the common labourer with contempt.

Peasantry

If labourers were considered a low form of life, the rural peasantry were regarded as little short of inhuman. Looked down upon by everybody, their hatred was mainly aimed against a nobility constantly seeking to increase its feudal rights at their expense.

THE THREE SOCIAL ORDERS OR 'ESTATES'
THE CLERGY - AS A CORPORATE BODY THE CLERGY OWNED ROUGHLY ⅒TH OF THE LAND. WITH AROUND 130,000 MEMBERS IT CONSISTED OF NOBLES AND BOTH UPPER AND LOWER BOURGEOIS.
THE NOBILITY - ESTIMATED BY SIÈYES AT 110,000 MEMBERS (BUT PROBABLY CLOSER TO 400,000) THE NOBILITY AS A WHOLE OWNED AROUND ⅕TH OF THE LAND. MANY IMPOVERISHED NOBLES HOWEVER, THEMSELVES OWNED BARELY ENOUGH TO PROVIDE EVEN A MEAGRE LIVING.
THE 3RD ESTATE - FROM RICHEST BOURGEOIS TO HUMBLEST PEASANT, EVERY BODY ELSE (SOME 25½ MILLION PEOPLE) WAS LUMPED TOGETHER IN THE THIRD AND LOWEST ORDER.

The Economic Crisis

The rise of central government and the emergence of an impersonal state machinery inevitably created an administrative potential which far exceeded available financial resources. The need for new revenue could only be met by increased taxation; but the French tax system was already overly-complicated and unjust.

Direct Taxation.

The Taille – theoretically imposed equally on all commoners but in reality collected from individuals in the north and from landed estates in the south.

The Poll Tax and the Twentieths – payable by everyone but easily avoided by the clergy and nobility.

The Corvée – a tax in labour on highways imposed arbitrarily on peasants who lived nearby.

Indirect Taxes – rights of collection were leased from the state by a company of 'Farmers General'. Methods of collection differed from place to place, producing a system of monstrous complexity and inefficiency.

TURGOT – CONTROLLER GENERAL OF FINANCES 1774–76

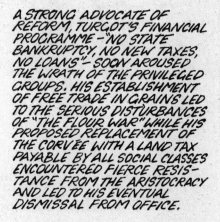

A STRONG ADVOCATE OF REFORM, TURGOT'S FINANCIAL PROGRAMME – "NO STATE BANKRUPTCY, NO NEW TAXES, NO LOANS" – SOON AROUSED THE WRATH OF THE PRIVILEGED GROUPS. HIS ESTABLISHMENT OF FREE TRADE IN GRAINS LED TO THE SERIOUS DISTURBANCES OF "THE FLOUR WAR" WHILE HIS PROPOSED REPLACEMENT OF THE CORVÉE WITH A LAND TAX PAYABLE BY ALL SOCIAL CLASSES ENCOUNTERED FIERCE RESISTANCE FROM THE ARISTOCRACY AND LED TO HIS EVENTUAL DISMISSAL FROM OFFICE.

The Financial crisis

A steady rise in population combined with bad harvests to produce severe unemployment. With the bourgeoisie holding on to their money, hoping to buy their way into the nobility, France's industrial growth developed too slowly to take up the slack. The rapid industrial growth of England provided serious competition to traditional areas of French commerce (e.g., the cloth industry).

1730-1789 – Food prices increase by an average of 48% to 65%, while wages increase by only 11% to 26%.

1790 – Arkwright's water frames in use in England numbered over 200, while in France there were only 8.

NECKER – RESPONSIBLE FOR FRENCH FINANCES 1776-81

A GENEVAN BANKER, NECKER'S FINANCIAL POLICY RESTED ALMOST SOLELY ON HIS ABILITY TO BORROW MONEY FOR THE STATE. TO MAINTAIN THE CONFIDENCE OF STATE CREDITORS HE ISSUED THE 'COMPTE RENDUE' – A FINANCIAL STATEMENT IN WHICH, BY OMITTING WAR COSTS, HE WAS ABLE TO REPORT AN APPARENT SURPLUS OF MORE THAN TEN MILLION LIVRES. THE PUBLICATION IN THE SAME REPORT OF THE AMOUNTS SPENT ON PENSIONS TO COURTIERS MADE NECKER IMMENSLY POPULAR WITH THE COMMON POPULACE BUT EARNED HIM THE HATRED OF THE ARISTOCRACY WHO AGITATED SUCCESSFULLY FOR HIS DISMISSAL.

AS A FOREIGN PROTESTANT NECKER COULD NOT LEGALLY BE GIVEN THE TITLE OF CONTROLLER GENERAL DESPITE THE FACT THAT HE EXERTED ALL THE POWER OF THAT OFFICE.

The Institutional crisis

France's outward appearance as a powerful centralized state concealed a confused and mismanaged administrative system which was rapidly approaching the point of collapse.

The second half of the 18th century saw the emergence of the French 'parléments' or high courts as the chief instrument of resistance to royal authority. Claiming to speak for the nation, the Paris and provincial parléments were in fact the weapons with which the nobility hoped to regain control of government. The royal provincial agents of 'Intendants' were themselves members of the nobility and as such divided in their loyalties and unwilling to take strong measures against the increasingly belligerent parléments.

1 The King – Absolute ruler by divine right.
2. The Ministers – 7 in all. Nominated by the King.
3. the Intendants – 32 in all. Local agents nominated by the King.
4. Local Administration
5. The provincial états – composed of clergy, nobility and upper bourgeoise. Their chief function was the assignment of taxes.
6. The Church
7. The peasantry
8. Tax Officials – appointed by the King: they were ironically called the élus or 'elected'. They assigned taxes to those provinces which had not maintained their representative assemblies of
 • 'états'.
9. The seigneur
10. The local courts
11. The parléments – 14 provincial parléments and the Paris Parlément whose area of jurisdiction exceeded that of any of the provincial parléments. Enjoyed considerable administrative powers, the most significant being the registration of new acts of royal legislation. Members bought or inherited their posts which conferred noble status.
12. The Councils – 4 in all. Nominated by the King.

The Enlightenment

The many phases of the Enlightenment – a revolution in philosophy characterizing the 18th Century and of special importance to France – can be simplified into 3 main trends of thought.

1. Closely linked to the ideas of Locke and Montesquieu, asserting that govenment is based on a contract between King and subjects and should consist of 3 separate powers: legislative, executive and judicial.

2. Voltaire and the physiocrats, happy enough with absolute monarchs so long as they were 'enlightened' but rejected Montesquieu's appeal to historic rights and invoked instead the concept of natural rights as a weapon against privilege.

3. Rousseau and his followers who found mankind perverted by civilization and called for a return to primitive simplicity and equality, entailing the destruction of privilege and the limitation of property.

ROUSSEAU

LA HARPE

CONDORCET

D'ALEMBERT

19

THE REVOLT OF THE NOBLES

In 1783, with the financial crisis being met by forced loans and the partial repudiation of state debts, Calonne was appointed Controller General of Finances. For 3 years he was content to follow Necker's policy of borrowing wherever possible; but by 1786 government credit was completely exhausted. The only alternatives open were either bankruptcy or total reform of the financial structure.

Calonne's solution was to propose the abolition of the existing tax system and its replacement by a single Universal Land Tax.

To forestall resistance from the parléments, an extraordinary assembly of notables was convened in 1787 and asked to approve the new proposals. When the assembly refused to countenance the land tax, Calonne was dismissed from office and replaced by the leader of the assembly, Brienne.

To the consternation of the notables, Brienne presented them with virtually the same proposals for reform, which they once again rejected, demanding in effect the summoning of the Estates-General (a body representing all the social orders, last held in 1614) to settle the matter. At Brienne's request the King dissolved the assembly of notables and the proposed reforms were taken directly before the parléments or 'sovereign courts'.

The Paris parlément, speaking for both itself and the 14 provincial parléments, accepted the many administrative reforms which Brienne advanced, but remained fiercely hostile to the crucial question of tax reform which they saw as an attempt to destroy the privileges of the higher orders.

THE PARLÉMENT INSISTS THAT IT IS DEFENDING 'THE RIGHTS OF THE NATION'.

IF I GIVE WAY THE MONARCHY WILL BE NO MORE THAN AN ARISTOCRACY OF MAGISTRATES.

AND IS LOUDLY ACCLAIMED BY THE PEOPLE OF PARIS.

AUGUST 14TH – THE EXILE OF THE PARLÉMENT TO TROYES LEADS TO RIOTING IN PARIS.

NOVEMBER 19TH – RECALLED TO PARIS FOR AN EMERGENCY 'ROYAL SESSION', THE PARLEMENT IS SURROUNDED BY TROOPS AND FORCED TO APPROVE URGENTLY NEEDED LOANS.

IT IS LEGAL BECAUSE I WISH IT.

A RASH ASSERTATION OF THE ROYAL PREROGATIVE WHICH COULD ONLY LEAD TO FURTHER UNREST.

THE NEXT 6 MONTHS SEE AN INCREASE IN CIVIL DISTURBANCES – THE WORST INCIDENT IS AT GRENOBLE, WHERE THE 'DAY OF THE TILES' (MAY 8TH) LEAVES 4 DEAD AND 30 INJURED.

AAACHO

SEEKING SUPPORT FROM THE BOURGEOISIE, THE NOBLES REDOUBLE THEIR DEMANDS FOR AN ESTATES GENERAL. BUT ON JULY 21ST AT VIZILLE, A MEETING OF REPRESENTATIVES OF THE 3 ORDERS CALLS FOR DOUBLE MEMBERSHIP OF THE 3RD ESTATE. IN THE FACE OF THIS UNEXPECTED DEVELOPMENT, THE UNEASY ALLIANCE BEGINS TO BREAK UP.

JULY/AUGUST A 'PAMPHLET WAR' BREAKS OUT AS THE UNEASY ALLIANCE BETWEEN NOBILITY AND BOURGEOISIE BEGINS TO BREAK UP — THE MOST POWERFUL PUBLICATION TO EMERGE IS SIEYES 'WHAT IS THE THIRD ESTATE?'

AUGUST 24TH — BRIENNE DISMISSED AND REPLACED BY NECKER.

QU EST-CE QUE LE TIERS ETAT?

MAY 5TH 1789 — THE ESTATES GENERAL FINALLY CONVENES.

What did the nobles really want?

The 18th Century saw the authority of the King extending further than ever before, as the State embarked on a desperate search for revenue. To prevent any erosion of their traditional privileges, the nobility had both to contain the growth of royal authority and place themselves in control of the state machinery. Resistance to the King would be far more effective if it was supported by the Third Estate, or at least that wealthy portion of the bourgeoisie which itself aspired to the nobility. The parléments were prepared to bring the Third Estate into the picture by demanding an Estates-General, so long as this posed no threat to the traditional organization of society. The wholly unexpected call for doubling of representation within the lower order alarmed the nobility and exposed the alliance for the sham it was.

The break between nobility and bourgeoisie provided the opportunity for a new alliance of King and commoner which might have saved France from the upheavals of the following years. Louis, however, was too firmly entrenched in traditional habits to do more than nod in the direction of the lower orders. The royal decision to accept double representation was rendered pointless by his refusal to sanction voting by heads rather than orders. The Third Estate were left to smoulder in resentment at their manipulation and rapid desertion by both King and privileged classes.

THE 'ENLIGHTENED' COURT

One member of the nobility on whose support Louis would be unable to count in the forthcoming struggle was his cousin Philippe, Duc d'Orléans. Devoted to mysterious intrigues, often so impenetratable as to defy description, he was to welcome the onset of Revolution as a useful vehicle for his own ambitions – the elimination of the house of Bourbon and his elevation to the throne. Dissipated and totally unprincipled, Philippe or his agents were never far from the centre of popular unrest, while his highly vocal support of the radical left during the power struggles of 1792/3 was to cause them considerable embarrassment. A dangerous nuisance and a constant reminder of the worst aspects

Prior to 1787, the Enlightenment in France existed as a purely intellectual debate confined mainly to the aristocracy. The primitivism of Rousseau held a particular fascination for those members of the court who, while they had no intention of sacrificing their personal advantages to the welfare of the community, as Rousseau demanded, could nevertheless transfer his vision of a simple rustic society into a suitably outrageous style of fashion. The effects of the Enlightenment were limited to certain members of the nobility dressing themselves as red Indians, or the appearance of court ladies with nests of live birds incorporated into their elaborate hairstyles.

The attempts of the nobility to gain the support of the bourgeoisie led to the first real dissemination of Enlightenment ideas outside the aristocracy, as the parléments resorted to the arbitrary use of Enlightenment jargon in the cause of political conservatism. The appeal to 'natural rights' was used to defend any demands which local circumstances made necessary and inevitably led to such absurd positions as, for instance, the insistence of the officials of Toulouse on 'the inalienable, imprescriptable, eternal and natural rights of municipial oligarchies'.

The ideas of the Enlightenment had been dragged from the rarefied world of the intellect and distorted to suit the needs of the conservative elements within French society. Their appearance in the real world brought them to the attention of that section of society which would later use them to provide an ideological justification of what was, in 1789 at least, primarily a social revolution.

of the aristocracy, the self-styled Philippe 'Egalité' was finally executed in 1793 by the Terrorist government, removing from the arena of the Revolution one of its least attractive, and in many ways, one of its most pathetic characters.

PARIS IN 1789

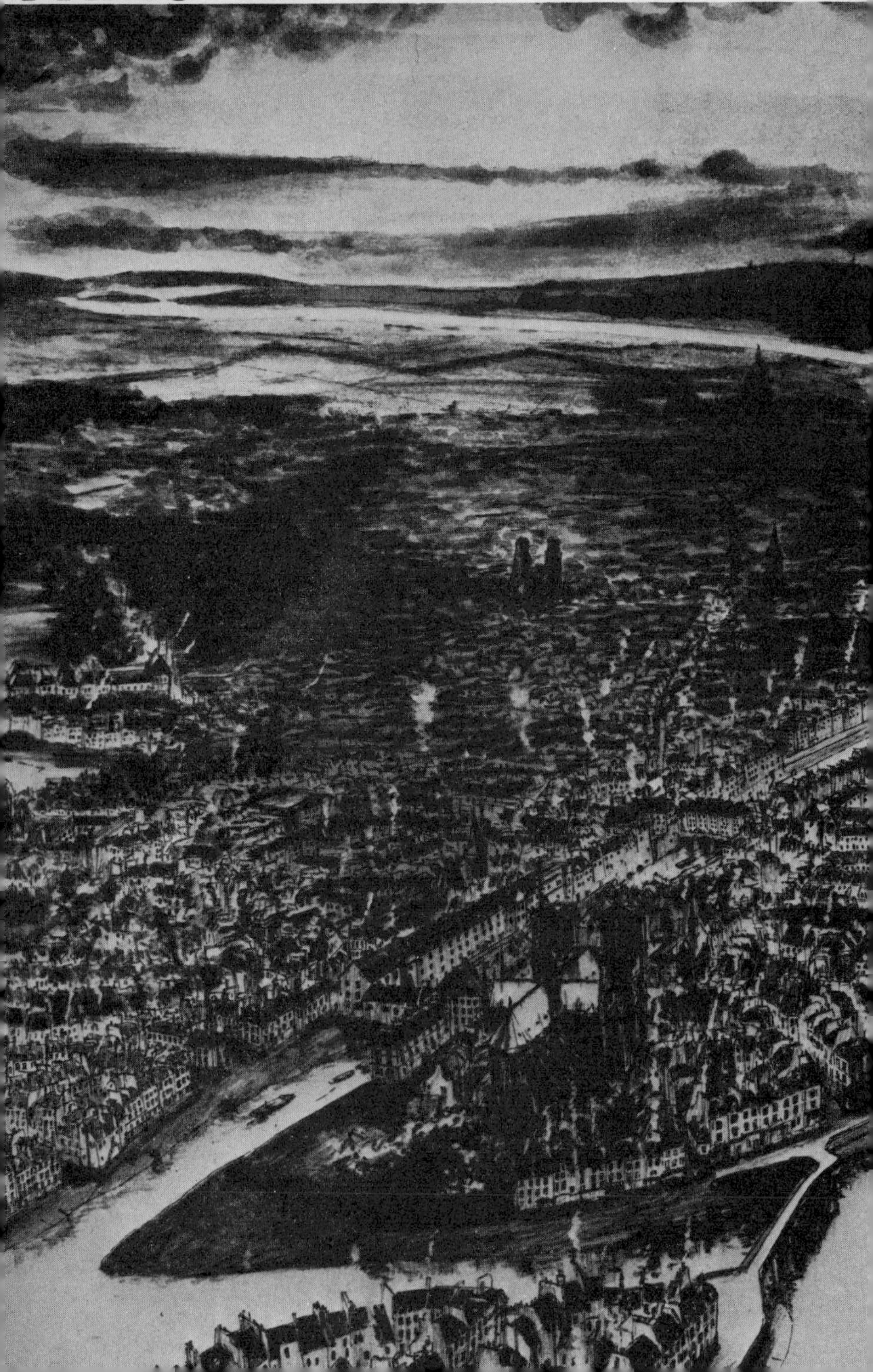

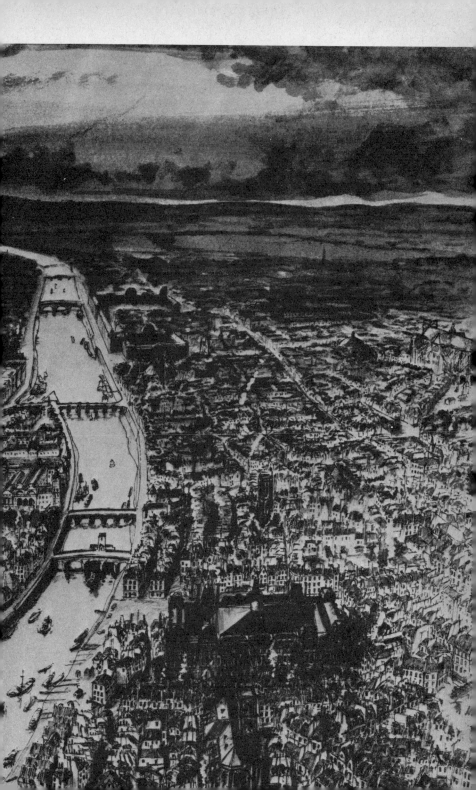

PARIS IN 1789

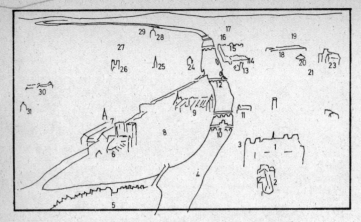

1 Hôtel de Ville, 2 St-Gervais-St-Protais, 3 Place de Grève,
4 Port au Blé, 5 Île St Louis, 6 Notre-Dame, 7 Hôtel-Dieu (hospital)
8 Île de la Cité, 9 Palais de Justice (law courts), 10 Pont Notre
Dame, 11 Le Châtelet (police headquarters and prison), 12 Pont Neuf
and Samaritaine, 13 St-Germain-l'Auxerrois, 14 Palais du Louvre,
15 Palais des Tuileries, 16 Jardin des Tuileries, 17 Champs-Elysées,
18 Palais Royal, 19 Faubourg St Honoré, 20 Halle au Blé (corn market)
21 Quartier des Halles, 22 St-Merri, 23 St-Eustache, 24 College des
Quatre Nations. 25 St-Germain-des-Prés, 26 St-Sulpice, 27 Faubourg
St-Germain, 28 Hôtel des Invalides (military hospital), 29 Champs
de Mars, 30 Palais du Luxembourg, 31 Sorbonne (university).

Paris, the main arena of the revolution, had a population of some
600,000 people. With the royal court long removed to Versailles, the
city was mainly devoted to commercial and financial interests, with
the bourgeoisie a well-established, dominant social group. Paris had
always jealously protected its pre-eminent position, with Parisians
resentful of royal interference, and never slow to meddle in the
affairs of France if neccessary. It has been accurately pointed
out by many historians that every King who ruled from Paris
eventually lost his throne. This fact was recognized by the greatest
of the French monarchs, Louis XIV, who had moved his court to the
less threatening environs of Versailles. The unfortunate Louis XVI
was not to find isolation from Paris quite so easy.

The view on the preceding pages looks westwards across the centre
of Paris toward the affluent residential areas of the Faubourgs St.
Honoré and St Germain. Some amenities and activities of an
eighteenth-century city can be traced along the river Seine. In the
foreground, close to the Hôtel de Ville, is the Porte-au-Blé
where much of Paris' grain supplies arrived by boat. Beyond lies the
Pont de Nôtre-Dame, with its water pump for supplying the
surrounding area. On the Seine itself, several laundry barges can be
distinguished.

Above and below; The Quartier des Halles

PARIS IN 1789

The governing body of Paris was housed in the Hôtel de Ville, a squat rennaissance building fronted by the Place de Grève, so called because here Parisians traditionally presented their grievances to the city authorities. To the east of this point lay the area known as the Marais, once a fashionable residential area but by 1789 merely a sad jumble of decaying mansions and squalid tenements. Dissecting the Marais ran the Rue St -Antoine, at the end of which loomed the Bastille, marking the easternmost point of the old city boundary. Beyond this notorious fortress was the Faubourg St -Antoine, which then as now, was a centre of furniture manufacturing. This area was to be at the forefront of popular activity during the revolutionary period. With a large population of skilled artisans, performing much the same jobs for similar pay and conditions, the Faubourg was invested with a strong sense of common identity, equalled only by the inhabitants of the Halles (markets) district.

Right: A furniture workshop in the Faubourg St-Antoine.

Below: The Bastille. In the foreground, part of the Marais. To the right is the Arsenal quarter; while to the left, beyond the Bastille, is the Faubourg St-Antoine.

PARIS IN 1789

Furniture workers considered themselves among the élite of the work-force, earning double the wages of a labourer or porter. Among the lowest paid were the bakers' assistants, considered "a breed of wild and savage cavemen", and whose employers were thought to be little better. A considerable proportion of the lower-paid had come to Paris from other parts of the country to the dingy chambres garnies common in central Paris.

There are some instances of workers and craftsmen organizing to strike for better pay and conditions; but it was more usually the price of food, and particularly that of bread, which caused the most concern. In times of shortage, the price of bread could rise sharply. When in 1789 the cost of a loaf rose from 8 to 14½ sous, this fact, far more than the impending Estates General, occupied the attention and anxieties of the ordinary people of Paris. The Estates General was not to see the end of such problems but the start of a decade of dearth, inflation and misery, on a scale previously unknown in eighteenth-century France.

Chapter Two

THE VICTORY OF THE THIRD ESTATE

QU'EST-CE QUE

LE TIERS-ETAT?

Le plan de cet Ecrit est assez simple. Nous avons trois questions à nous faire.

1°. Qu'est ce que le Tiers-Etat? Tout.

2°. Qu'a-t-il été jusqu'à présent dans l'ordre politique? Rien.

3°. Que demande-t-il? A y devenir quelque chose.

On verra si les réponses sont justes. Nous examinerons ensuite les moyens que l'on a essayés, & ceux que l'on doit prendre, afin que le Tiers-Etat devienne, en effet, *quelque chose*. Ainsi nous dirons:

4°. Ce que les Ministres ont *tenté*, & ce que les Privilégiés eux-mêmes *proposent* en sa faveur.

5°. Ce qu'on auroit *dû* faire.

6°. Enfin ce qui *reste* à faire au Tiers pour prendre la place qui lui est due.

THE ESTATES GENERAL

The Third Estate posed a considerable threat to the King and privileged classes. Regarding itself as 'the nation', it implicitly rejected the existence of any other order. By achieving double membership of the Estates General, it had guaranteed its own success in any vote taken by head rather than order. Already several liberal noblemen had broken the traditional barriers between orders by forming a 'Patriot' party with members of the bourgeoisie. The burning question of the day was whether the King could enforce the traditional method of voting by estates, placing the Third Estate at the mercy of the combined voting-power of the higher orders.

1ST ESTATE INCLUDED A GOOD PROPORTION OF PARISH PRIESTS SYMPATHETIC TO THE 3RD ESTATE.

3RD ESTATE REPRESENTED THE VAST BULK OF THE NATION BUT PROPERTY QUALIFICATIONS AND AN INDIRECT SYSTEM OF VOTING MADE IT EXCLUSIVELY BOURGEOIS AND LARGELY UPPER-BOURGEOIS'.

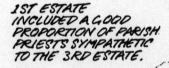

WHAT IS THE THIRD ESTATE? – EVERYTHING.

WHAT HAS IT BEEN HERETOFORE IN THE POLITICAL ORDER? –NOTHING.

WHAT DOES IT DEMAND? – TO BECOME SOMETHING THEREIN.

SIÈYES – "QU'EST-CE QUE LE TIERS ÉTAT?"

2ND ESTATE ALL BUT A HANDFUL VIOLENTLY OPPOSED TO SOCIAL CHANGE.

The formation of the National Assembly

From the outset, the refusal of the Third Estate to constitute itself as a separate order brought proceedings to a standstill. Threatened with Royal intervention, they adopted a proposal by Sieyés calling on the other orders to join them, while on the 17th of June they conferred the title of National Assembly upon the combined orders. Three days later, finding themselves locked out of their hall, the Third Estate met at an indoor tennis court and there took the famous 'Tennis Court Oath', swearing not to separate until a constitution had been established.

On the 23rd, the King addressed the Estates, threatening to dissolve the Assembly if they refused to separate. The clergy and nobles withdrew, but the Third Estate refused to disperse. Louis' unwillingness to test the truth of Mirabeau's assertion that the members would not stir unless forced by bayonets, let to most of the clergy and 47 nobles joining the Assembly. Four days later the King reluctantly ordered the remaining delegates to do the same. A committee was quickly appointed to draw up a constitution and on the 9th of July the National Assembly became the Constituent Assembly.

The King Strikes Back

With the arrival at Paris of sixteen regiments, consisting largely of foreign mercenaries, the King appeared to be preparing for a military overthrow of the Assembly. This impression was reinforced when, on July 11th, Necker was suddenly dismissed from office and replaced by the ultra-conservative Baron de Breteuil.

Uncertain as to the future of the Assembly, the Paris bourgeoisie took steps to safeguard their own position. Meeting at the Hôtel de Ville, the electors of the Parisian deputies established the National Guard…

…a bourgeois militia with which they hoped to resist the King, while at the same time controlling and directing the civilian population.

Paris in alarm

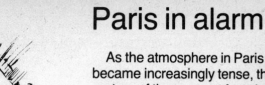

As the atmosphere in Paris became increasingly tense, the orators of the moment found a responsive audience among the worried citizens. At the gardens of the Palais Royal, Camille Desmoulins – the future 'Attorney General of the Lamp-post', called upon the populace to take up arms against the forces of reaction.

Determined to put down disorder, the Royal cavalry attacked demonstrators at the Place Louis XV and were themselves attacked by companies of Gardes-Françaises sympathetic to the cause of the Third Estate. Resistance to the King was further encouraged by the destruction of the hated customs posts surrounding the city.

With the police showing no desire to tangle with the crowd, disturbances spread rapidly throughout Paris. Sword- and gunsmiths' premises were ransacked in a frantic search for arms and ammunition until finally, in desperation, the crowd turned for help to the self-proclaimed municipal authorities. Besieged at the Hôtel de Ville, the newly formed permanent committee of electors, in the shape of the Provost of Merchants, de Flesselles, proved decidely unhelpful. Alarmed by the dangerous mood of the people, he attempted to divert them toward the arsenal of the Invalides.

On the morning of July 14th, the Invalides was invaded and more than 28,000 muskets captured, but precious little powder or cartridges. In need of a source of ammunition, the attention of the crowd became centred on the fortress of the Bastille…

41

THE FALL OF THE BASTILLE

Called upon to hand over the fortress to a citizens' militia, the commanding officer, de Launey, proved fatally indecisive. As the excited crowd gathered beneath the walls, the panic-stricken garrison opened fire and battle began. The result remained uncertain, until the arrival among the attackers of French and National Guardsmen equipped with cannon captured from the Invalides. Faced with an artillery barrage, de Launay gave way and threw open the gates. But with close to 100 of their number dead, the crowd was in no mood to accept such a tardy surrender. De Launay was dragged from the Bastille, and hacked to death outside the Hôtel de Ville. His severed head, together with that of the obstructive de Flesselles, being paraded through the city.

The Bastille was stormed in order to obtain ammunition and not, as popular mythology would try to insist, out of any particularly strong desire to release its prisoners. The infamous dungeons had long since fallen into disuse, and at the time of the attack those unfortunates lodged within the building itself numbered only seven: four forgers, two lunatics (including a demented Irishman believing himself to be Julius Caesar and God) and a nobleman imprisoned under a 'lettre de cachet' for incest. With the fortress already scheduled for demolition, the significance of the attack lay more in its psychological rather than actual effects. Strategically positioned at the edge of the troublesome Faubourg St-Antoine, the Bastille served as both a symbol and constant reminder of the arbitrary power of the King. In its fall, the people of Paris saw the collapse of the old and, until then, apparently unassailable regime.

LATE ON THE EVENING OF THE 14TH THE KING SAT DOWN AT VERSAILLES AND MADE A ONE-WORD ENTRY IN HIS DIARY

RIEN...*

*NOTHING

BUT EVEN LOUIS COULD NOT MAINTAIN SUCH A FICTION FOR LONG.

Unable to count on the support of his troops, Louis dispersed the recently arrived regiments and reluctantly reinstated Necker. On July 17th, at the Hôtel de Ville, he symbolically accepted the tri-color emblem of the revolution and appeared on the balcony to tumultuous applause from the assembled citizenry.

On the evening of August 4th, several liberal noblemen acting at the instigation of the Breton deputies, rose to announce to the Assembly their voluntary renunciation of traditional privileges. Initial displeasure soon gave way to a mood of sweeping enthusiasm, bordering on hysteria, as nobility, clergy and representatives of parléments and privileged towns joined them in the wholesale discarding of long-established rights.

The bewilderment of the conservative elements within the Assembly was adequately conveyed by the reaction of the Marquis Lally Tollendal…

As might be expected, many delegates soon regretted their hasty promises, and during the next few days the effect of the 'evening of sacrifices' was considerably qualified. The Assembly had decreed 'the abolition in its entirety of the feudal regime'. But with the worst of the feudal dues made subject to redemption, the dismantling of the system still lay somewhere in the future. Nevertheless, the August decrees had achieved their purpose; the old system was destroyed in principle, and in anticipation of promised reforms, the great fear evaporated as quickly as it had arrived.

On August 26th the Assembly adopted a Declaration of Rights largely drawn up by Lafayette, the hero of the American War of Independence…

The French Declaration of Rights differed dramatically from its American predecessor in its refusal to limit itself to any specific country or system of government. It is this universal nature which gave the document much of its prestige and popularity. Applicable with equal facility either to monarchy or republic, the Declaration was in reality nothing less than a bourgeois manifesto. Liberty and equality are set forth as inalienable rights, with as much emphasis, if not more, placed on the sanctity of property. The Declaration was the creation of a class who had come to power, and intended to stay there. Relying heavily on the notion of a 'will of the nation', expressed through and embodied in the representatives of that nation, the Declaration shuns direct democracy, replacing the tyranny of the privileged classes with an equally powerful tyranny of the bourgeoisie.

MARIE JOSEPH DU MOTIER, MARQUIS DE LAFAYETTE (1757-1834).

DESPITE HIS COMMITMENT TO SOCIAL CHANGE LAFAYETTE WAS NONE THE LESS A ROYALIST AT HEART AND ABOVE ALL, DESIROUS OF PERSONAL POWER. DURING THE CONSTITUTIONAL MONARCHY, LAFAYETTE'S COMMAND OF THE NATIONAL GUARD MADE HIM POTENTIALLY THE MOST POWERFUL MAN IN FRANCE. HIS ABILITY, HOWEVER, NEVER QUITE MATCHED HIS AMBITION AND BY 1792 HIS CONTRIBUTION TO THE REVOLUTION WAS OVER. HE WAS TO SPEND SEVERAL YEARS IN AN AUSTRIAN PRISON BEFORE RETURNING TO FRANCE IN 1802.

THE GREAT FEAR

The shock waves of the King's capitulation spread rapidly throughout France. Old municipal authorities either prudently came to terms with new revolutionary committees or were simply removed by force. Royal authority was no longer recognized and existing citizen militias were soon absorbed into the National Guard. As central authority collapsed, the provincial bourgeoisie, while theoretically agreeing to respect the decrees of the National Assembly, found themselves able to exercise absolute power over their own districts as they saw fit. With the conclusion of mutual assistance pacts between neighbouring municipalities, France became, in effect, a loose federation of individual communes. But local autonomy brought its own problems. Problems which were about to transform the countryside into a theatre of violent unrest.

RUMOUR - FOREIGN INVASIONS

DURING THE PERIOD OF THE FEAR REPORTED SIGHTINGS OF FOREIGN TROOPS BECAME COMMONPLACE. THE BRITISH FLEET WAS SEEN OFF BREST, POLISH TROOPS AT DUNKIRK, SPANIARDS AT BORDEAUX AND AUSTRIANS ON THE ROAD TO LYONS. THROUGHOUT FRANCE ANYTHING THAT MOVED WAS LIKELY TO BE INTERPRETED AS AN INVASIONARY FORCE.

SUMMER 1789

Administrative change did little to help the peasant who was still crippled by manorial taxation, while the expulsion of beggars and vagabonds from the towns only increased the vast numbers of jobless roaming the countryside. In the wake of demands for free pasturage and removal of enclosures, a series of agrarian riots broke out. With them came the extraordinary upsurge of rumour and counter-rumour, which became known as the great fear. The fear proved highly contagious: everywhere peasants fled their homes, châteaux and tax offices were burned, nobles and town officials shot, stabbed or lynched on the traditional instrument of summary justice, the lamp-post. In Paris, the more radical members of the Assembly became convinced the only way to re-establish control over the provinces was by a carefully prepared attack on the feudal system itself.

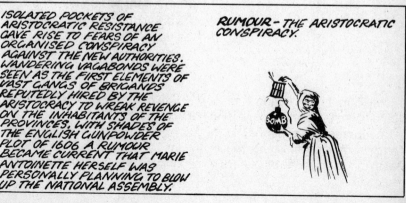

ISOLATED POCKETS OF ARISTOCRATIC RESISTANCE GAVE RISE TO FEARS OF AN ORGANISED CONSPIRACY AGAINST THE NEW AUTHORITIES. WANDERING VAGABONDS WERE SEEN AS THE FIRST ELEMENTS OF VAST GANGS OF BRIGANDS REPUTEDLY HIRED BY THE ARISTOCRACY TO WREAK REVENGE ON THE INHABITANTS OF THE PROVINCES. WITH SHADES OF THE ENGLISH GUNPOWDER PLOT OF 1606 A RUMOUR BECAME CURRENT THAT MARIE ANTOINETTE HERSELF WAS PERSONALLY PLANNING TO BLOW UP THE NATIONAL ASSEMBLY.

RUMOUR - THE ARISTOCRATIC CONSPIRACY.

BOMB

Louis' refusal to approve either the August decrees or the Declaration of Rights posed a serious threat to the Assembly's fragile unity.

Incensed by the casual rejection of their work, the Patriot party demanded the King be given only a suspensive veto on certain legislative matters.

BARNAVE

DUPORT

LAMETH

CLERMONT-TONNERE

LALLY TOLLENDALL

ROLE OF THE KING

LEGISLATIVE VETO ONLY

ABSOLUTE VETO

Against them stood those 'Monarchials' or 'Anglomaniacs' who believed the revolution had already gone far enough. Fully supporting the King's right of veto, they also favoured the introduction of an upper house for the aristocracy, along the lines of the English parliamentary model.

The Patriots proved the more persuasive of the two groups, and the decrees were returned to the King 'for acceptance only'.

Encouraged by dissent within the Assembly, Louis chose to ignore its demands and signalled his own intentions by recalling the troops to Paris. Once again, fears of a Royal conspiracy hovered over the city.

October 1st, Versailles. – At a banquet held in honour of the newly arrived Flanders regiment, the over-enthusiastic guests hurled a stream of insult and invective at the revolution and its leaders. The Royal family were loudly acclaimed and tri-color cockades discarded in favour of the white of the Bourbon dynasty.

The activities of the inebriated revellers gave Desmoulins and his fellow orators exactly the ammunition they had been looking for.

Exaggerated accounts of the 'Versailles Orgy' soon gave rise to the demand that the King be brought to Paris where he could be isolated from the corrupting influence of the court.

"October days"

On October 5th angry crowds of women gathered at the Hôtel de Ville to demonstrate against the price of bread. Persuaded to petition the King directly, they set out for Versailles, where they were joined by the National Guard under Lafayette. Receiving only vague promises from the King, the crowd attacked the palace during the night and several of the royal bodyguard were slain before the National Guard managed to restore order.

With the courtyards ringing to the cry "Le Roi à Paris", Louis reluctantly agreed to accompany Lafayette to the capital. On the afternoon of the 6th, the royal family was removed to Paris escorted by what one royalist observer described as, "a drunken and ferocious troop of furious men and women without modesty, several bearing the dismembered heads of the unfortunate bodyguard". With the King safely housed in the Tuileries, the Assembly soon installed itself nearby.

HONORÉ RIQUETTI,
CONTE DE MIRABEAU
(1749-91).

TECHNICALLY A NOBLE BUT
ELECTED TO THE ESTATES
GENERAL AS A MEMBER OF
THE 3RD ESTATE, MIRABEAU
PROVED AN EXCELLENT
ORATOR AND RAPIDLY
BECAME ONE OF THE MOST
SIGNIFICANT FIGURES
WITHIN THE ASSEMBLY.
REFERRED TO AFFECTIONATELY
BY THE PEOPLE AS 'THE
LITTLE MOTHER' MIRABEAU
WAS IN FACT A NATURAL
INTRIGUER, EASILY BRIBED
AND PRONE TO CHANGIING
HIS POSITION AS HIS
PERSONAL AMBITION
DIRECTED. HIS DEATH IN
APRIL 1791 CAME JUST IN
TIME TO SAVE HIS
REPUTATION FROM
COMPLETE DESTRUCTION.

The Jacobin Club

Originally known as the Breton Club, the better-known name derived
from the convent of the Jacobin friars at whose premises the
Society met in Paris. Initially a meeting place for Deputies of the
patriot party, the Club was soon the centre of a network of
affiliated Societies throughout France. Fairly moderate at the
beginning of the Revolution, the Club soon became a focus for
more revolutionary activity. By 1792, the Club had become the crucial
link between the radical members of the Assemmbly and the rapidly
burgeoning popular movement. After this date, the term 'Jacobin'
generally reflects a radical political stance rather than indicating actual
members of the Club.

Chapter Three

THE CONSTITUTIONAL MONARCHY

Having achieved, in principle, the destruction of the old regime, the Assembly now set about the task of creating a new system compatible with the ideas expressed in the Declaration of Rights.

the work of the CONSTITUTIONAL MONARCHY

Administration

With the communal councils thrown up by the municipal revolution a fait-accompli, the Assembly was happy enough to build on an already existing structure. France was divided into 83 Departments sub-divided into districts and communes, each with its own council. Judicial functions were separated from administration, and both town officials and judges were elected rather than appointed. Equality before the law became a fact and the bug-bear of the Ancien Régime, venality of office, was abolished. The tentative assistance pacts of 1789 blossomed into provincial leagues or 'Federations', while the King's authority became legally non-existent. He was no longer King of France, merely 'King of the French'.

Sale of land

The indemnification of the majority of manorial dues was a bitter blow to the peasantry, mostly unable and unwilling to pay the required redemption fees. Similarly, the sale of nationalized land promised much but delivered little. Instead of fixed and affordable prices, land was sold in large blocks at open auction. This method ensured that, except for rare instances where peasants combined to outbid single buyers, land passed mainly to farmers with already existing holdings. The peasants were left to the mercy of speculators who bought land to divide for re-sale. This unfortunate policy inevitably led to a considerable decline in revolutionary enthusiasm among the agrarian population.

An interesting side-note is the fact that this period saw the first use of the terms 'left' and 'right' as applied to politics. It is ironic that seating arrangements within the Constituent, with radicals to the left of the president and conservatives to the right, should provide the Assembly with probably its most enduring contribution to posterity.

Economics

Committed to economic freedom, the Assembly nevertheless moved slowly in this area owing to a populace still strongly attached to controls. Internal customs barriers, tolls and checkpoints were removed, but protection against foreign competition continued. Demands for price controls were firmly refused.

Taxation

Indirect taxation was completely abolished. Old direct taxes were replaced by taxes on moveable property, commercial and industrial revenue and the 'patriotic contribution' which called for 25% of each person's income. A new land tax was instituted, but administered largely through guesswork, pending a national land survey.

Finance

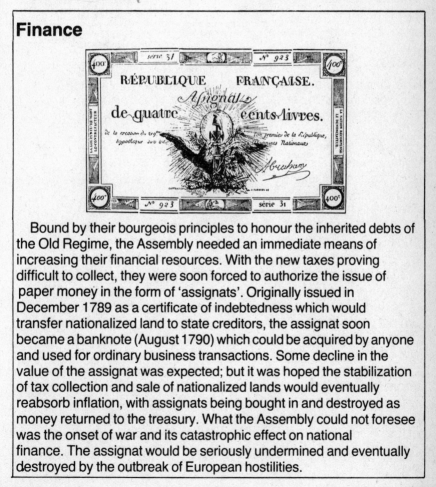

Bound by their bourgeois principles to honour the inherited debts of the Old Regime, the Assembly needed an immediate means of increasing their financial resources. With the new taxes proving difficult to collect, they were soon forced to authorize the issue of paper money in the form of 'assignats'. Originally issued in December 1789 as a certificate of indebtedness which would transfer nationalized land to state creditors, the assignat soon became a banknote (August 1790) which could be acquired by anyone and used for ordinary business transactions. Some decline in the value of the assignat was expected; but it was hoped the stabilization of tax collection and sale of nationalized lands would eventually reabsorb inflation, with assignats being bought in and destroyed as money returned to the treasury. What the Assembly could not foresee was the onset of war and its catastrophic effect on national finance. The assignat would be seriously undermined and eventually destroyed by the outbreak of European hostilities.

THE CONSTITUTIONAL MONARCHY AND THE CHURCH

PIUS VI

The nationalization of church lands (Nov. 1789) and the suppression of religious orders (Feb. 1790) had already destroyed much of the independence of the church. The Civil Constitution of the clergy (July 1790) attempted to make the remaining church organization an extension of the state by adapting it to the administrative framework. Bishops and priests alike would become little more than civil servants, elected to office and obliged to take an oath of loyalty to the constitution. The primacy of the Pope would be retained but his authority would no longer be recognized.

With the Pope silent on the matter, Louis was persuaded to approve the Civil Constitution. But Pius VI had merely postponed his verdict, and in March 1791 he roundly condemned both the Civil Constitution and those precepts contained within the Declaration of Rights.

The consternation aroused by the Pope's outburst took the Assembly completely by surprise. Steeped in the anti-clericalism of the 'philosophes', they had failed to see that among the traditionally devout peasantry the fear of eternal damnation was likely to prove far stronger than the bonds of revolutionary loyalty. As it became clear that the constitutional clergy could, in many parishes, only be imposed by force, a strange situation was allowed to develop with jurors (those priests who had taken the oath) and non-jurors (those who refused to do so) existing side by side, and in some cases even conducting their separate services in the same churches. The problem of non-juring priests was to be a constant thorn in the side of the Assembly and was to provoke increasing criticism from the citizens of Paris.

Meanwhile, the King's refusal to co-operate with the Assembly was a source of continuing anxiety for many of its members. The result was to be two years of intrigue which seriously undermined the authority of many prominent revolutionaries.

While monarchists and moderates alike were ruining their reputations in vain attempts to come to terms with the King, France and Paris in particular was experiencing a sudden groundswell of popular political activity, clearly observable in the sudden explosion of new political clubs and societies.

While the already established Jacobin Club (formerly the Breton Club) had primarily served as a focus for the radical bourgeoisie within the assembly, new clubs such as the Cordeliers (founded April 1790) and the Indigents (founded March 1791) attracted a wider spectrum of membership among ordinary citizens who desired a more active say in the nation's political life. In a similar manner, the birth of numerous popular societies, such as Claire Lacombe's Society of Revolutionary Women, provided new opportunities for sections of society previously isolated from political debate.

The emergence of the lower classes into the political arena was convincingly demonstrated by the unparalleled flood of popular pamphlets and newspapers which characterized the period. The best known of these publications, such as Marat's *L'Ami du peuple* or Hébert's *Père Duchesne* were literally only the tip of an immense iceberg.

LE BABILL.

JOURNA

DU PALAIS- RO.AL

LE PATRIOTE FRANÇOIS,
JOURNAL LIBRE, IMPARTIAL ET NATIONAL
Par une Société de Citoyens, & dirigé par J. P. BRISSOT DE WARVILLE

Une Gazette libre est une sentinelle qui veille sans cesse pour le Peup

To the upper bourgeoisie, the revolution appeared complete. Self-congratulation seemed to be in order, and a series of elaborate festivals were held to celebrate national unity. The most impressive of these was the 'Fête de la Fédération', held at Paris on July 14th, 1790, to commemorate the anniversary of the storming of the Bastille. Crowded into the Champ de Mars, thousands of provincial National Guardsmen joined the King, Assembly members and citizens of Paris in swearing undying loyalty to the nation.

But as the political consciousness of the people expanded many of the bourgeois politicians began to retreat more and more into the rarefied world of the Paris Salons. The salons undoubtedly offered a useful forum for discussion, and the best known of them, that of Madame Roland, was to provide that enigmatic woman with the opportunity of exercising considerable political power. But it was in the clubs and societies that new political ideas were surfacing, and any politician who ignored the clubs ran the risk of losing touch with public opinion, while forfeiting his ability to influence local activity.

E BABILLARD,

L'AMI DU PEUPLE
OU
LE PUBLICISTE PARISIEN,

OURNAL POLITIQUE ET IMPARTIAL,
r M. MARAT, Auteur de L'OFFRANDE A
A PATRIE, du Moniteur, et du PLAN
CONSTITUTION, etc.

No. 37.

JOURNAL

DU DIABLE.

Je me suis constitué l'ange-gardien de la nation.

PARIS IN 1790

In May 1790 Paris was divided into 48 sections for civil and administrative purposes. These sections soon developed extra political functions in the shape of clubs and local assemblies. Increased activity at a local level was gradually to give the crowd a more precise identity than it had ever previously possessed – an identity which was to prove crucial in the upheavals to come.

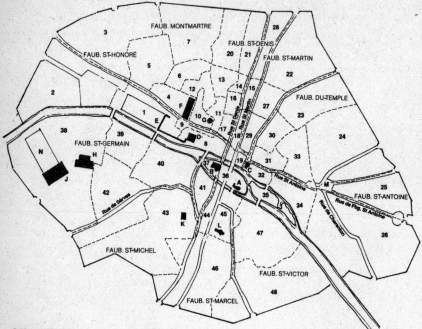

A Notre Dame
B Palais de Justice
C Hôtel de Ville
D Louvre
E Tuileries and
   Tuileries gardens
F Palais Royal
G Corn Market (Halle
   au Blé)
H Invalides
J École Militaire
K Palais de
   Luxembourg
L Ste Géneviève
   (re-name the
   Panthéon in 1791)
M Place de la Bastille
N Champ de Mars

THE PARIS SECTIONS
1790
(later names in brackets)

1. Tuileries
2. Champs-Élysées
3. Roule (Republique)
4. Palais Royal (butte des
   Moulins, Montagne)
5. Place Vendôme
   (Piques)
6. Bibliothèque
   (Lepeletier)
7. Grange Batelière
   (Mirabeau, Mont-
   Blanc)
8. Louvre (Muséum)
9. Oratoire (Gardes
   Français)

10. Halles au Blé
11. Postes (Contrat Social)
12. Place Louis XIV (Mail,
    Guillaume Tell)
13. Fontaine Montmorency
    (Molière et la Fontaine,
    Brutus)
14. Bonne Nouvelle
15. Ponceau (Amis de la
    Patrie)
16. Mauconseil (Bon
    Conseil)
17. Marchés Des Innocents
    (Halles, Marchés)
18. Lombards
19. Arcis
20. Faubourg Montmartre
    (Fbg. Mont-Marat)

Who were the Sans-Culottes?

The term Sans-Culotte, referring to those who wore trousers rather than the knee breeches of the wealthy, was originally applied in a purely social sense to the small traders, wage earners and vagrants of both town and country. During the revolution the term became more commonly applied to the politically active within these classes and was usually extended to include the more radical agitators of the period regardless of their social background. Active in both the Paris Commune (the title given to the new Paris local government) and the sections, the Sans-Culottes were to form the power base with which the popular politicians were to back their demands for radical policies.

The Democratic Movement

The years 1789-91 saw the growth of a new political movement among the lower classes. Originating among those to whom the debating floor of the Assembly was denied, the democratic movement soon gained adherents within the Constituent itself. During this formative period, the demands of the movement's spokesmen usually stopped short of outright Republicanism; although as early as 1790, a few of their number, such as Robert in his paper *Le Mercure National,* were proclaiming their support for Republican ideals.

HEBERT
POPULAR
JOURNALIST

DESMOULINS
ORATOR

DANTON
MEMBER OF THE
PARIS COMMUNE

BRISSOT
EDITOR OF
'PATRIOTE
FRANCAIS'

MARAT
POPULAR
JOURNALIST

ROBESPIERRE
MEMBER OF THE
CON'ST ASSEMBLY

The democratic movement was to cover a wide spectrum of political opinion and would at no time coalesce into a political party in the modern sense. Increasingly prone to internal division, the movement would constantly find itself split into several factions, often revolving around no more than one or two main figures.

THE CONSTITUTION OF 1791

After 2 years of preparation, the Constituent Assembly finally presented the nation with a constitution.

The Constitution of 1791 dealt a shattering blow to the principles of democratic sovereignty. Citizens were divided into 'active' and 'passive' citizens, dependent on the amount of tax they paid, while stiff property qualifications ensured that only the propertied classes would elect members to or take seats within the new Assembly. With considerable justification, the leaders of the democratic movement accused the Assembly of creating 'an aristocracy of wealth'.

1789 "DEMOCRACY"   1791 "MERITOCRACY"

With its appointed task complete, the Constituent dissolved itself on September 30th, 1791, in preparation for the election of the new Legislative Assembly.

Seriously alarmed by the rapid growth of the democratic movement, many members of the Constituent had found themselves siding with the reactionary aristocrats, or 'Blacks', against more radical politicians. These moderates, led by Lafayette and the Triumvirate of Duport, Lameth and Barnave, now decided that the work of the Constituent needed careful review. The democratic impulse had to be checked by the introduction of even more stringent property qualifications, suppression of clubs and censorship of the press. To achieve these aims, they had to keep themselves in power by being re-elected to the Legislative Assembly. When, largely due to the influence of Robespierre, members of the Constituent were declared ineligible for election to the new Assembly, these ex-moderates began to assume an increasingly reactionary position. In the summer of 1792 two unexpected and totally shattering events were to bring matters to a head . . .

FLIGHT TO VARENNES

ON THE EVENING OF JUNE 20th 1791 A SHADOWY GROUP OF FIGURES FURTIVELY BOARDED A WAITING COACH AT THE TUILERIES. WITH THE HELP OF SWEDISH NOBLEMAN, VON FERSEN, THE KING HAD FINALLY DECIDED TO FLEE FROM FRANCE.

HURRY SIRE, LOYAL TROOPS ARE WAITING FOR US AT THE BORDER.

BUT AT THE SMALL TOWN OF VARENNES

HALT!

THE OCCUPANTS OF THE CARRIAGE WERE QUICKLY IDENTIFIED, PLACED UNDER ARREST AND ESCORTED BACK TO THE CAPITAL BY THE NATIONAL GUARD.

CONTEMPORARY ACCOUNTS AGREE THAT AS THE ROYAL PARTY RE-ENTERED PARIS THE ASSEMBLED CROWDS FELL INTO A STRANGE, ALMOST FUNEREAL, SILENCE — AND INDEED FOR MANY OF THE ONLOOKERS, THE INCIDENT MUST HAVE MARKED THE DEATH OF ANY REMAINING TRACES OF LOYALTY TOWARDS THE KING AND THE BEGINNINGS OF A NEW COMMITMENT TO THE IDEALS OF REPUBLICANISM.

ON JULY 17th A LARGE CROWD GATHERED AT THE CHAMP DE MARS TO SIGN A REPUBLICAN PETITION DRAWN UP BY THE CORDELIERS CLUB. AS THE PROCEEDINGS BEGAN TWO UNFORTUNATES DISCOVERED BENEATH THE CENTRAL PLATFORM WERE IMMEDIATELY DENOUNCED AS ROYALIST SPIES AND SUMMARILY LYNCHED.

FEARING A RIOT THE PERMANENT COMMITTEE DISPATCHED LAFAYETTE AT THE HEAD OF THE NATIONAL GUARD.

WHEN THE CALL TO DISPERSE PRODUCED NO RESPONSE FROM THE CROWD THE GUARDSMEN RECEIVED THE ORDER TO....FIRE!

With more than fifty demonstrators dead at the Champ de Mars, the Patriot party found itself irreparably split into two distinct groups.

The Feuillants – Constitutional monarchists composed mainly of ex-Jacobins who had left in protest at a petition to dethrone the King.

The Democrats – Drawn largely from the Cordeliers and remnants of the Jacobin Club within the Democratic ranks, Republicans were becoming increasingly influential.

THE MONARCHIALS

LAMETH

BARÈRE

DUPORT

BARNAVE

LAFAYETTE

SPIRIT OF REPUBLICANISM

THE FEUILLANTS

ROBESPIERRE

JACOBIN CLUB

HÉBERT

DANTON

MARAT

CORDELIERS, CLUB

Enjoying immense support in the provinces, the Feuillants were also by far the largest group within the Assembly. But it was the Democrats who could count on popular support in Paris, and it was in Paris that the fate of the revolution would be decided.

THE GIRONDE

The elections to the legislative assembly saw no real change in the balance of seats, but marked the formation of a new political faction which was shortly to become the spearhead of the Republican movement. The deputies belonging to this faction were called 'Brissotins', but the group is more popularly referred to as 'the Gironde' after the department from which many of its members came.

GUADET CONDORCET GENSONNE BRISSOT VERGNIAUD PÉTION ROLAND MADAME ROLAND

GOD SAVE THE KING ~ IF HE KEEPS HIS WORD

Jacques Pierre Brissot (1754–93) – Few members of the new Assembly can have enjoyed such impeccable revolutionary credentials as the leader of the Girondins. The son of a humble inn-keeper, Brissot had been both an agent for the anti-slavery society and for a time, a prisoner in the Bastille. A free-lance journalist, his travels in several countries including America, gave him a spurious reputation for expertise in foreign affairs. Despite these advantages, Brissot's lack of foresight coupled with his impulsive and often irresponsible nature were to prove fatal defects for a man whose influence was to have a far-reaching effect on the course of the Revolution.

Pierre Vergniaud (1753-93) – If Brissot was the brain of the Gironde, Vergniaud was its most able voice. An exciting and persuasive speaker when roused, his sporadic bursts of brilliance were rendered all the more remarkable when contrasted to his usual attitude of lethargy and indifference. Quiet and withdrawn by nature, he was content to leave decision-making to his more forceful colleagues

69

Europe and the Treaty of Pillnitz

The monarchies of Europe had been watching events with growing unease; but it was not until Varenne and Louis' arrest that they felt compelled to take some form of action. The result was the Treaty of Pillnitz, issued by Austria and Prussia on August 27th, 1791, which called on the powers of Europe to prepare to intervene to restore the French monarchy if necessary.

BRITAIN'S ATTITUDE, LIKE THAT OF THE GERMAN STATES, WAS ONE OF CAUTION RATHER THAN OUTRIGHT HOSTILITY.

THE LOW COUNTRI SCENE OF A RECENT UPRISING AGAINST TH HADSBURGS, WERE OPENLY SYMPATHETIC

BRITAIN

IRELAND

LOW COUNTR

FRANCE

SPAIN

Discord between the states of Europe and internal strife considerably weakened the effectiveness of the Treaty. When Louis was restored to the throne, the powers were happy enough to let matters rest. The implied threat, however, remained.

DESPITE THEIR DECLARED OPPOSITION TO THE REVOLUTION BOTH PRUSSIA AND AUSTRIA WERE MORE CONCERNED WITH CATHERINE THE GREAT'S DESIGNS ON POLAND.

RUSSIA

PRUSSIA

GERMAN STATES

POLAND

SWITZERLAND

AUSTRIA

THE PAPACY

OTTOMAN EMPIRE

Amidst a growing feeling that the gains of the revolution would be lost, unless the enemies within and beyond the borders of France were swiftly eliminated, the Gironde began to demand not so much a war as a crusade against the crowned heads of Europe.

In October, the Gironde succeeded in passing several decrees against those émigrés who had fled to neighbouring countries. Louis firmly refused to sanction the decrees and the Gironde was forced to adopt another tack. On November 29th, they persuaded the Assembly to request that Louis order the elector of Trèves, a small town in Belgium under French rule, to disperse the armed companies of émigrés who were gathering there. Louis' compliance with the request would in effect reverse his veto and open the way for war against the émigrés and those countries who harboured them. The success of the Girondin tactic was assured by the unexpected support of Lafayette and his followers who were able to persuade the King to agree. The incident marked the beginning of a tacit alliance between the Gironde and Lafayette, which can only be understood by considering why two such disparate groups should desire the same result – *War!*

WAR!
FOR AND AGAINST

"WAR! THE PEOPLE ARE READY."

THE GIRONDE - GENUINELY BELIEVED THAT WAR WOULD SEE A GENERAL UPRISING AGAINST THE MONARCHS OF EUROPE

"BUT YOU! REPRESENTATIVES OF THE PEOPLE, ARN'T YOU READY TOO?... AND WHAT ARE YOU DOING ABOUT IT, IF YOU KNOW NOTHING BETTER THAN TO DELIVER THE PEOPLE TO THE TERRIBLE LAW OF INSURRECTION."

ROBESPIERRE - FORESAW THE TERRIBLE ECONOMIC BURDENS, THE DANGERS OF CIVIL WAR AND THE INEVITABLE SLIDE TOWARS DICTATORSHIP.

"THE IMBECILES THEY DON'T SEE THAT THIS SERVES OUR PURPOSES. INSTEAD OF CIVIL WE WILL HAVE POLITICAL WAR AND FRANCE WILL BE MUCH BETTER FOR IT."

THE KING - HOPED FOR AN AUSTRO-PRUSSIAN VICTORY AND THE RESTORATION OF HIS AUTHORITY.

"IT IS VERY INTERESTING TO START A REVOLUTIONARY WAR, BUT HARDER TO BRING IT TO ITS CONCLUSION."

BARNAVE - FEARED THAT WAR COULD ONLY BE OF BENEFIT TO THE LEFT.

LAFAYETTE - HOPED THAT A SHORT WAR WOULD ENABLE HIM TO RETURN WITH A VICTORIOUS ARMY, CRUSH THE RADICALS AND RULE FRANCE IN THE KINGS NAME.

In March 1792, Girondin intimidation forced the resignation of the King's ministers. Balancing his own desire for war against his antipathy toward the party, Louis appointed to the ministry a group of men closely connected with the Girondins.

Supporters of the Gironde crowded the new Cabinet, but in reality they occupied posts which carried little power. Apart from a few token Jacobins, the remaining ministers were patently the King's men. To Robespierre and the more radical revolutionaries, this compromise with the forces of reaction constituted a betrayal for which the Gironde was never to be forgiven.

THE TWO MOST PROMINENT GIRONDINS WERE THE OPPORTUNIST DUMOURIEZ (MINISTER OF WAR) AND THE INDUSTRIOUS BUT INEFFECTIVE ROLAND (MINISTER OF THE INTERIOR).

DUMOURIEZ

ROLAND

Confident that he could isolate Austria, take Belgium quickly and conclude an early peace, Dumouriez issued an ultimatum to the Emperor demanding that he reduce his armaments. With no reply forthcoming from Vienna, the cabinet proposed a declaration of war. On April 20th, the Assembly voted for war against the King of Hungary and Bohemia, i.e., Austria and not the Holy Roman Empire.

Chapter Four

THE ESTABLISHMENT OF THE REPUBLIC

THE WAR WAS NOT THE SUCCESS THE GIRONDE AND LAFAYETTE HAD HOPED....

I MUST THINK AGAIN... HOW COULD I HAVE HAD FAITH IN THIS RABBLE.

WE MUST RETIRE ANOTHER TEN MILES SIRE.

The optimism of the Gironde and their confidence in the revolutionary fervour of the troops were far outweighed by more material considerations. Arms and equipment were in short supply, distrust between officers and men endemic. The belief that the troops would receive their training through combat was never tested; at the first sight of hostile forces, the army was ordered to withdraw.

With the ranks thrown into confusion, withdrawal rapidly became headlong flight. At least one officer was murdered by his men, while another, more resolute than most, was forced to abort a bayonet charge when his troops voted against it. During the two-month campaign on the Belgian border, not one engagement would take place, and three regiments were to go over to the enemy. Lafayette himself would eventually desert to the Austrians; but in the meantime. he was about to execute a political about-face.

JUNE 1792 – THE GIRONDE RESORTS ONCE MORE TO THE POLICY OF INTIMADATION WHICH HAD BROUGHT THEM TO POWER.

JUNE 12th – ROLAND PUBLICLY CONDEMNS THE KING'S VETO OF THE DECREE AGAINST NON-JURERS AND HINTS AT THE POSSIBILITY OF DETHRONEMENT.

WE ARE BETRAYED BRISSOT LAFAYETTE HAS JOINED THE FEUILLANTS.

WE MUST REGAIN THE SUPPORT OF THE PEOPLE BY ATTACKING THE KING.

JUNE 13th – ROLAND AND THE OTHER GIRONDIN MINISTERS ARE REMOVED FROM OFFICE AND REPLACED BY FEUILLANTS.

GROS LOUIS, VOICI LES SANS-CULOTTES!

I AM STILL THE KING AND I WILL NOT BE DICTATED TO BY MY OWN MINISTERS.

MEANWHILE, THE MACHINATIONS OF THE GIRONDE SERVE ONLY TO ENFLAME THE PASSIONS OF THE SANS CULOTTES.

JUNE 20th – ARMED DEMONSTRATORS PENETRATE THE TUILERIES AND HARANGUE THE KING, FORCING HIM TO DON A LIBERTY CAP.

VIVE LA NATION!

OUI... VIVE LA NATION.

JUNE – JULY
PARIS BECOMES THE FOCUS OF INCREASING RUMOUR AND RECRIMINATION

IF YOU ASK ME THERE'S AN AUSTRIAN COMMITTEE AT WORK IN THE TUILERIES – WE SHOULD STOP THEM NOW BEFORE THEY COST US THE WAR.

LOUIS STILL REFUSES TO APPROVE THE DEPORTATION OF NON-JURING PRIESTS – HOW CAN WE FEEL SAFE WHEN THE KING CONTINUES TO PROTECT THE ENEMIES OF THE NATION.

AJESTÉS L'EMPEREUR ET LE ROI DE PRUSSE.

JME FERDIN
ANDANT-LES AR

R LA GRACE DE DIEU DUC DE BRUNSWICK ET

In July, the Duke of Brunswick, commander of the allied forces, issued a declaration threatening Paris with 'military execution and total destruction' in the event of violence being offered to the royal family. The reaction of the populace to this inflammatory document could only serve to exacerbate the ever-worsening situation.

JULY 2nd – FAILING TO REALIZE THAT THE INITIATIVE IS PASSING OUT OF THEIR HANDS THE GIRONDE OVERIDE A ROYAL BAN AND AUTHORIZE THE ARRIVAL AT PARIS OF THOUSANDS OF PROVINCIAL NATIONAL GUARDS (FÉDÉRÉS) FOR THE JULY 14th CELEBRATIONS.

THE ENCAMPED FÉDÉRÉS SOON FELL UNDER THE INFLUENCE OF THE MORE EXTREME PARIS DEMOCRATS... SUCH AS

SANTERRE.

BELATEDLY RECOGNIZING THAT THEY HAVE ENCOURAGED THE PRESENCE OF THOSE FORCES WHICH THEY CAN LEAST CONTROL, THE GIRONDINS ATTEMPT TO RECONCILE THEMSELVES WITH THE KING...

JULY 26th – BRISSOT THREATENS REPUBLICANS WITH THE FULL FORCE OF THE LAW AND ANNOUNCES HIS OPPOSITION TO DETHRONEMENT.

AUGUST – ISNARD REFERS CRYPTICALLY TO AN ORDER FOR THE ARREST AND TRIAL OF ROBESPIERRE.

AUGUST 4th – VERGNIAUD SUCCEEDS IN ANNULLING A DECREE OF THE MAUCONSEIL SECTION REFUSING TO RECOGNIZE LOUIS AS KING..

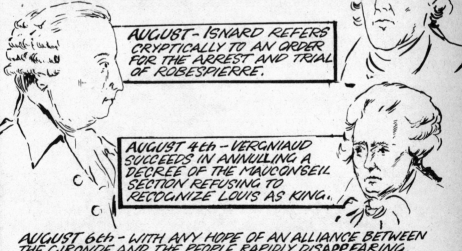

AUGUST 6th – WITH ANY HOPE OF AN ALLIANCE BETWEEN THE GIRONDE AND THE PEOPLE RAPIDLY DISAPPEARING, A MEETING OF FÉDÉRÉS AND SECTIONAIRES CALLS FOR THE IMMEDIATE ABDICATION OF THE KING. THE ST-ANTOINE SECTIONS GAVE THE ASSEMBLY UNTIL THE 9th TO IMPLEMENT THE PROPOSAL.

AUGUST 9th - AS IT BECOMES CLEAR THAT FAR FROM OBTAINING LOUIS' ABDICATION, THE ASSEMBLY HAS REFUSED EVEN THE LESSER DEMAND FOR THE INDICTMENT OF LAFAYETTE, ANGRY FÉDÉRÉS AND SANS-CULOTTES CONVERGE ON THE HÔTEL DE VILLE WHERE THE PARIS COMMUNE IS FORCIBLY DISBANDED AND AN INSURRECTIONARY COMMUNE INSTALLED.

WE PROTEST. YOU HAVE NO LEGALLY CONSTITUTED RIGHT TO INTERFERE WITH THE COMMUNE.

WE HAVE EVERY RIGHT! WHEN THE PEOPLE PLACE THEMSELVES IN A STATE OF INSURRECTION, THEY WITHDRAW ALL POWER FROM OTHER AUTHORITIES AND ASSUME IT IN THEMSELVES.

MANDATE, THE PRO-ROYALIST HEAD OF THE NATIONAL GUARD, IS MURDERED....

DONG
DONG
DO
DONG
DONG
DONG

....AND THE TOCSIN SOUNDS FOR THE SECOND REVOLUTION.

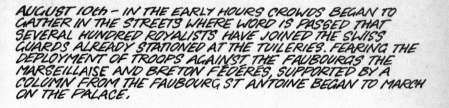

AUGUST 10th – IN THE EARLY HOURS CROWDS BEGAN TO GATHER IN THE STREETS WHERE WORD IS PASSED THAT SEVERAL HUNDRED ROYALISTS HAVE JOINED THE SWISS GUARDS ALREADY STATIONED AT THE TUILERIES. FEARING THE DEPLOYMENT OF TROOPS AGAINST THE FAUBOURGS THE MARSEILLAISE AND BRETON FÉDÉRÉS, SUPPORTED BY A COLUMN FROM THE FAUBOURG ST ANTOINE BEGAN TO MARCH ON THE PALACE.

ATTEMPTING TO FRATERNIZE WITH THE DEFENDERS THE FÉDÉRÉS ARE FIRED ON AND THE BATTLE FOR THE TUILERIES BEGINS....

ORDERED BY THE KING TO CEASE FIRE AND WITHDRAW, THE SWISS GUARD ARE OVERRUN BY THEIR ATTACKERS. OVER 500 ARE MASSACRED ON THE SPOT AND 50 MORE PUT TO DEATH AT THE HÔTEL DE VILLE.

THE KING FLEES TO THE ASSEMBLY BUILDING WHICH IS INVADED BY SANS-CULOTTES. ROBESPIERRE NOW EMERGES AS THE ARBITER OF FRANCES FATE.

WE MUST ELECT A NATIONAL CONVENTION. TO DRAW UP A NEW CONSTITUTION. A CONVENTION BASED ON UNIVERSAL SUFFERAGE. A CONVENTION OF THE PEOPLE.

SUSPENDED BUT NOT YET ABOLISHED, THE KING AND HIS HOUSEHOLD ARE CONFINED WITHIN THE GRIM MEDIEVAL FORTRESS OF THE TEMPLE.

PENDING THE ELECTION OF THE NEW CONVENTION, A PROVISIONAL EXECUTIVE COUNCIL IS ESTABLISHED — BRINGING TO PROMINENCE ONE OF THE MOST DYNAMIC MEMBERS OF THE PARIS COMMUNE, DANTON.

SEPTEMBER 2nd—6th — FEARS OF COUNTER REVOLUTION CAUSE WIDESPREAD ALARM AND THE REVOLUTIONARY MOOD OF THE PEOPLE ERUPTS ONCE MORE INTO VIOLENCE. WITH THE TACIT APPROVAL OF THE AUTHORITIES PRISONERS ROUNDED UP AFTER THE EVENTS OF AUGUST ARE SEIZED BY THE MOB AT PRISONS THROUGHOUT PARIS.

AIMED ORIGINALLY AGAINST POLITICAL PRISONERS THE DISTURBANCES SOON DEGENERATE INTO A SERIES OF BRUTAL AND INDISCRIMINATE EXECUTIONS. THESE SEPTEMBER MASSACRES ACCOUNT FOR OVER 1000 DEATHS— THE MAJORTY BEING ORDINARY COMMON LAW CRIMINALS

ELECTION OF THE CONVENTION— WITH THE MASSACRES KEEPING THE ROYALIST SYMPATHISERS AWAY FROM THE POLLS THE GIRONDE ARE RETURNED AS THE LARGEST SINGLE GROUP BUT MANY OF THE PARIS DEMOCRATS ALSO SECURE SEATS AND EMERGE AS AN IMPORTANT FACTOR IN THE CONVENTION: THIS NEW GROUP BECOMES KNOWN AS 'THE MOUNTAIN'.

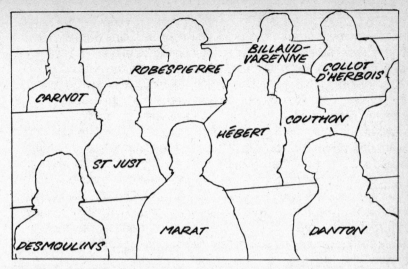

At this early stage of its existence, the two most important members of the Mountain were probably the popular journalists Hébert and Marat, both of whom could count on the support, respect and admiration of the Sans-Culottes.

Jacques René Hébert (1757–94) – The son of a goldsmith, Hébert's neat appearance and polite behaviour gave little outward sign of his talent for invective and abuse, often carried to incredible heights of vulgarity and obscenity. While his hatred for the monarchy as expressed in the pages of his paper, *Le Père Duchêsne*, gave him a large following among the Sans-Culottes, his poverty stricken past provided fertile ground for his enemies who accused him of being 'a liar and a thief'. It is interesting that, at his trial in 1794, many of the specific charges against him related to 'the theft of shirts and other sundry effects'.

Jean-Paul Marat (1743–93) – Unlike Hébert, Marat did not confine his attacks to the monarchy; a true democrat, he directed his considerable literary powers against almost everyone. An ex-physician, Marat was of an intense, nervous disposition. Suffering from a painful skin disease, he made his unpleasant appearance worse by deliberately wearing filthy clothes as a sign of his position as 'l'ami du peuple'. Shunned by his colleagues within the convention and constantly rebuked for his unceasing demand for 'blood and heads', he was nevertheless idolized by the Sans-Culottes. Venomous and unlikable, Marat was at least sincere in his championship of the people, and at the time of his murder, his personal fortune (unlike that of many other Deputies) consisted of one assignat to the value of 25 livres.

The Revolution of August 10th brought political democracy to France, but with the democratic process overshadowed by the September Massacres. The elections saw the disapperance of both Royalist and Feuillant from the political arena. (Universal sufferage not withstanding, members of the Feuillant Club at Paris were denounced as enemies of the Revolution and deprived of the right to vote.) Because of this, and in the light of future events, it is easily forgotten that the power groups now facing each other within the Convention were both parties of the left. The Gironde had, after all, blazed briefly as the spearhead of radical policy; but cursed with a positive genius for miscalculation, they now found themselves cast in the role of reactionary old guard, committed to the consolidation of an exclusively Bourgeois Revolution. While this might still find many adherents in the provinces, it was no longer compatible with the increase in awareness and political effectiveness of the Parisian crowd.

The democrats of the Mountain, in themselves no less bourgeois than the Gironde, were more keenly receptive to the demands of the people, and through their involvement with the Jacobin and Cordeliers Clubs, they undertook to act as intermediaries between the Sans-Culottes and the Convention. As the first days of the Republic dawned, the gulf between the parties was by no means insurmountable; but the Gironde had no consistent policy other than attack, and their blind hostility towards the new 'upstarts' was to leave the Mountain with little room for manoeuvre.

THE CORDELIERS CLUB

Named after the monastery of the Cordeliers where its members originally met, the Cordeliers Club had a lower subscription charge than the Jacobin Clubs and generally attracted a more extreme membership. Situated in the Theatre Française Section on the left bank, the club had numbered amongst its members such figures as Danton and Marat. After the second Revolution many of its more prominent members found the policy of 'out jacobining the Jacobins' too extreme for their tastes and withdrew, leaving the club largely in the control of the Hébertists and Enragés (cf. chapter 5).

Chapter Five

THE GIRONDE AND THE MOUNTAIN

The Gironde, the Mountain...

Within the convention, the Mountain now stood in direct opposition to the Gironde. With support drawn largely from the Paris sections, and enmeshed in an uneasy alliance with the Sans-Culottes, the Montagnards emerged, perhaps not altogether willingly, as the representatives of the 'men of August' and their ideals.

The Gironde, with support in the provinces and the full weight of the upper bourgeoisie behind them, were undoubtedly the stronger party. But without the support of the large number of uncommitted delegates (known as 'the Plain' or more unkindly, 'the Marsh') neither group could effectively dominate the other. The members of the Plain were essentially opportunists. Bourgeois, they instinctively sided with the Gironde, but were always ready to transfer

that support to the Mountain should the Gironde show signs of becoming too strong.

The Convention's first action had been to abolish the monarchy and usher in Year I of the Republic. They were immediately faced with demands for the trial of the King. Many Girondins, fearing the advantage that such a trial would give to the extremists, and the

....and the Plain

inevitable repercussions abroad, found themselves caught between two evils. They could not oppose a trial without seeming to condemn the events of August and the Convention in which they themselves sat, while to condone it would lose them the support of the moderates and leave them isolated. In an attempt to postpone the issue, the Gironde launched itself into all out attack on the Mountain.

Attempts were made to indict both Marat and Robespierre as 'aspirant dictators', but the Plain, disturbed by the prospect of an all-powerful Gironde, gave its support to the Mountain and the charges were dropped.

On November 20th an iron chest was discovered at the Tuileries. In it was found the King's secret correspondence with Austria. The compromising nature of these papers ensured that the trial of the King could no longer be postponed. On December 11th, Louis was finally brought before the Assembly to answer charges of 'having committed various crimes to re-establish tyranny on the ruins of liberty'.

The trial of the King

In the context of revolutionary France, Louis was patently guilty of the charges brought against him. After a vain attempt by his defence to invoke royal inviolability, he was found so by a unanimous verdict. The only question open to debate was whether he should suffer the death penalty. An attempt by Brissot and Vergniaud to avoid the necessity of voting on the issue, by calling for a national referendum, came to nothing and the fatal vote was called on January 16th.

A majority of the members declared in favour of the death penalty; but several of those doing so also called for a stay of execution and an examination into the possibility of a reprieve. The Gironde, still hoping that the King's life could be saved, called for a re-vote on reprieve; but the death sentence was once again returned, this time by an even greater majority than before. On both occasions, the Girondin vote had split, exposing once and for all the disorganization of the party.

Meanwhile, the Sans-Culottes in the public galleries were making a careful record of the names of the 'Appellants' or members who had called for a reprieve.

ON JANUARY 21ST 1793 AT ABOUT 9:30 A.M. LOUIS XVI WAS EXECUTED AT THE PLACE DE LA REVOLUTION (ONCE KNOWN AS THE PLACE DE LOUIS XV,)
IN THE LIGHT MORNING RAIN. THE FULL ENORMITY OF THE OCCASION BEGAN TO SINK HOME UPON THE ASSEMBLED CROWDS. THE UNTHINKABLE HAD BEEN DONE - FRANCE WAS NOW A NATION OF REGICIDES.

Compared to previous methods of execution in France, the guillotine was actually a distinct improvement. Owing its name, but not its existence to Dr Joseph Guillotin, through whose efforts the privilege of decapitation had been extended to all social classes rather than just the aristocracy, it was a relatively quick and humane means of dispatch. Although new to France, the guillotine had long been known ir other countries, one such machine being noted as the penalty for sheep stealing in Halifax by the Elizabethan antiquary, William Camden. The French guillotines were in fact made to order by German contractors and constructed under the strict supervision of the Academy of Surgeons.

Along with the new Convention, the autumn of 1792 gave France her first taste of military success.

THE PRUSSIANS DEFEATED VALMY – SEPT. 20TH

THE AUSTRIANS DEFEATED JEMAPPES – NOV. 6TH

November 19th – The Convention issues the decree of Fraternity and Help, offering aid to all peoples desirous of overthrowing their monarchs and conveniently paving the way for the annexation of Savoy and the 'Republicanization' of Belgium.

On November 16th, a French fleet had forcibly re-opened the Scheldt estuary, closed to all but Dutch shipping for over 150 years. Allied to Holland, British neutrality began to waver. The decree of fraternity and the Convention's expressed intention to expand the nation to its 'natural limits' (i.e. The Rhine frontier) saw a rapid deterioration in diplomatic relations, while the execution of the King provided Pitt with a useful pretext for war.

'IF FRANCE IS REALLY DESIROUS OF MAINTAINING FRIENDSHIP AND PEACE WITH ENGLAND, SHE MUST SHOW HERSELF DISPOSED TO RENOUNCE HER VIEWS OF AGGRESSION AND AGGRANDISMENT, AND TO CONFINE HERSELF WITHIN HER OWN TERRITORY....

....UNLESS SHE CONSENTS TO THESE TERMS, WHATEVER MAY BE OUR WISHES FOR PEACE, THE FINAL ISSUE MUST BE WAR.'

Having counted on British neutrality, the Convention was momentarily nonplussed, but with public opinion firmly behind the extension of the war they soon overcame their misgivings. On February 1st, the convention pre-empted the British Prime Minister, voting for a declaration of war against both England and Holland. Spain was added to the list on March 7th.

Until the execution of the King, one of the few critics of the Revolution in Britain was Edmund Burke author of the trenchant Reflections on the Revolution.

'IF THE PRESENT PROJECT OF A REPUBLIC SHOULD FAIL, ALL SECURITY TO A MODERATE FREEDOM MUST FAIL WITH IT.'

In response to Burke, Thomas Paine wrote his great eulogy of the Revolution – The Rights of Man. *Increasingly isolated from British public opinion, Paine was to emigrate to France and take up an active role in politics there.*

The First Coalition

Orchestrated by Britain, the First Coalition was a formidable force on paper, but in reality its war aims were hopelessly diverse. Neither Prussia nor Austria were to pursue the war with sufficient effort, and all the powers involved proved overly-concerned with their own interests.

BRITAIN ACTED AS PAYMASTER TO THE COALITON, FINANCING THE MASSIVE CONTINENTAL ARMIES.

BRITAIN

SPAIN

FRANCE

THE SPIRIT OF FRENC. DEFIANCE WAS ENCAPSULATED BY TI ENERGETIC FIGURE OF DANTON.

In this respect, Britain was by far the worst offender, greedily concentrating her forces on those French colonies whose loss could have no direct impact on the defeat of the Republic. Nevertheless, as the spring campaign opened the coalition was soon enjoying considerable success.

PRUSSIA

RUSSIA

£

POLLAND

POLAND

AUSTRIA

VOLTAIRE

DESPITE HER ANTIPATHY TO THE REVOLUTION CATHERINE REMAINED NEUTRAL, CONCENTRATING HER ENERGY ON THE PARTITION OF POLAND IN COLLUSION WITH PRUSSIA AND AUSTRIA.

THE MISERY OF FRANCE / SPRING 1793

Food shortages become acute as the war with Britain disrupts imports. Inflation continues to soar and the French economy collapses.

The outbreak of civil war seriously affects internal distribution of available food supplies.

Defeated at Neerwinden (18th March) and Louvain (20th March) Dumouriez tries to lead the army in a coup against Paris. When his battered forces refuse to follow him, he deserts to the enemy.

CIVIL WAR IN THE VENDEE

The attempted conscription of men between the ages of 20 and 40, together with the harsh treatment handed out by many local authorities to the non-juring clergy, provoked widespread resentment in the provinces. In March, a series of uprisings broke out among the peasantry of the Vendée with many of the main towns being overrun and their Republican administrators massacred. The disturbances spread rapidly throughout western France.

Anti-Republican elements quickly assumed control of the uprisings, dividing the area among themselves and establishing a rudimentary government. The situation soon escalated into civil war as the convention sent the National Guard against the insurgents. The failure of the Guardsmen to quell the rebellion, and the reluctance of the Convention to divert troops from the frontier, allowed the leaders of the insurrectionary forces time to establish their authority. Eventual deployment of front-line troops achieved only limited success. Within the Vendée itself the insurgents were not to suffer any serious defeat until as late as October, Charette, one of the most important Vendéan leaders, was not to come to terms with the Republican authorities until 1795.

The inability of the Vendéans to maintain any form of permanent or unified army ensured that the revolt remained comparatively localized. But the continuing failure of the authorities to pacify the region hindered both trade and troop movements, and served as a constant pointer to the shortcomings of the policy of decentralisation which the Gironde had adopted and encouraged.

THE ENRAGES

The Gironde now found themselves under increasingly vocal attack from a group of extremists known as *les Enragés* or 'madmen'.

The demands of the Enragés were well received by the Sans-Culottes and popular journalists such as Hébert and Marat. The Montagnards, however, proved more difficult to convince. To the members of the Mountain, demands based on a social rather than political programme seemed little more than irrelevant, while the call for price controls struck hard against their bourgeois principles of economic freedom. Nevertheless, the need to maintain the support of the Sans-Culottes and the opportunity to isolate the Gironde proved irresistible, and the Mountain deemed it prudent to adopt the demands for their own ends.

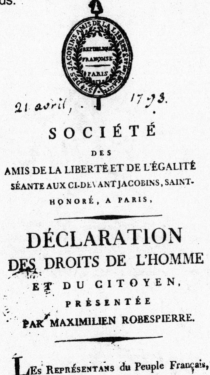

21 avril, 1793.

SOCIÉTÉ

DES

AMIS DE LA LIBERTÉ ET DE L'ÉGALITÉ

SÉANTE AUX CI-DEVANT JACOBINS, SAINT-

HONORÉ, A PARIS,

DÉCLARATION

DES DROITS DE L'HOMME

ET DU CITOYEN,

PRÉSENTÉE

PAR MAXIMILIEN ROBESPIERRE.

LES REPRÉSENTANS du Peuple Français,
réunis en Convention Nationale,

A

Assailed from all sides, the Gironde baulked at the wholesale abandonment of free trade and decentralisation; but in an attempt to stem the growing tide of unrest some proposals were grudgingly carried out. Provincial watch committees were set up to oversee local authorities; a maximum price was instituted on grain and fodder; and a revolutionary tribunal established to try enemies of the revolution and thus hopefully forestall any repetition of the September massacres.

If the Gironde expected their half-hearted measures to impress the Sans-Culottes, they were sadly mistaken. Far more important was the fact that the Gironde had already compounded their unpopularity by launching attacks on both Danton and Marat.

ACCUSED OF COMPLICITY IN DUMOURIEZ'S TREASON DANTON, IN ONE OF HIS MOST BRILLIANT SPEECHES, DEFLECTS THE CHARGE BACK OUT TO THE GIRONDE.

ARRAIGNED BEFORE THE REVOLUTIONARY TRIBUNAL, MARAT (NOW THE PRESIDENT OF THE JACOBIN CLUB) IS RECEIVED AS A HERO AND INSTANTLY AQUITTED.

On April 6th, the ascendent Danton was able to exert pressure on the Convention to create a Committee of Public Safety with himself as its most prominent member. The powers at the disposal of this body, for the moment extremely limited, were soon to exceed even the wildest dreams of its creator.

Alarmed by their unpopularity within Paris, the Gironde turned to the provinces for support. Their appeal found a ready response among Republicans hostile to the more extreme democrats, bourgeois monarchists and supporters of the non-juring clergy; all of whom rushed to hide themselves behind the handy label of 'Girondin'. Meanwhile, in Paris, the Commune began to see itself as the target of a vast conspiracy directed by the Girondin party.

Matters came to a head when the Paris Commune resolved to form a revolutionary army. The plan was denounced to the Convention, and on May 24th a Girondin commission appointed to investigate the affair ordered the arrest of 4 Sans-Culottes, including both Varlet and Hébert.

THE FALL OF THE GIRONDE

On the 27th, a large crowd surrounded the Tuileries, invaded the Convention hall and successfully demanded the suppression of the Girondin commission and the release of the prisoners. Later that evening, an insurrectionary committee of Sans-Culottes was formed.

On June 2nd an impressive demonstration was staged before the Tuileries, while inside, members of the insurrectionary committee demanded the arrest of those 'appellant' deputies who had voted against the execution of the King. The Convention members attempted to leave the hall but were stopped by the National Guard who had surrounded the palace. Returning to their places both the right, with great reluctance, and the Mountain, with obvious enthusiasm, acceded to the demands of the demonstrators and ordered the arrest of 29 deputies, nearly all of whom were leading Girondins.

SUPREMACY OF THE MOUNTAIN

With the Gironde broken, the Mountain now became the dominant force within the Convention. As such, they were anxious to ensure their authority was not undermined by the insurrectionary committee which had catapulted them to their new position. This tricky problem was resolved when the committee allowed itself to be disbanded following the offer of 40 sous a day in compensation for loss of earnings to those Sans-Culottes who had taken part in the demonstrations of May and June.

But if the Sans-Culottes were prepared to be bought off so easily, because they believed themselves to have the type of government which they had always desired, they were soon to be disillusioned. The fate of the arrested Girondins remained undecided, the anticipated revolutionary army was not formed and the Mountain appeared unwilling or unable to exercise its new power.

The inactivity of the Mountain contrasted sharply with the speed with which events delivered a series of body blows to the nation during the months of June to August. Girondin agitation provoked a series of anti-Jacobin or 'federalist' revolts in the provinces, while continuing defeats on the frontiers were capped by the fall of Toulon to the British. Food riots broke out in Paris and on July 13th, Marat, the hero of the Sans-Culottes, was murdered by a young Girondist, Charlotte Corday.

The 'martyrdom' of Marat stunned Paris. Spurred by popular indignation the sleeping Mountain erupted into sudden near-hysterical activity. The Committee of Public Safety was reorganized with the increasingly moderate Danton ousted and replaced by Robespierre. Marie Antoinette was sent to trial. The devastation of the Vendée was ordered, while a revolt at Lyons was put down with ruthless severity. All British subjects were subjected to arrest, Pitt was officially proclaimed 'the enemy of the human race', and the entire population of France was called to arms in a levy 'en masse'.

To the Sans-Culottes the actions of the Mountain still fell far short of their most important demands – a controlled economy and the ruthless elimination of all anti-revolutionary elements. On September 4th they took matters into their own hands. The Hôtel de Ville was invaded and a revolutionary commune was formed. The following day, demonstrators surrounded the Convention and forced it to make terror 'the order of the day'.

During the following weeks, the Mountain formally embarked on its new policy by admitting extremist deputies (Billaud-Varrenne and Collot d'Herbois) to the Committee of Public Safety, passing the 'Law of Suspects' (17th) which defined suspected persons so vaguely that no-one could count themselves entirely safe, and fixing prices to a general maximum (29th).

Georges Jacques Danton 1759-94 – Ugly, loud and imposing, Danton's spectacular rise from relative obscurity to political predominance in 1792 was the result of his unflagging energy and oratorical brilliance. But while Danton's prestige was immense, his reputation for venality and his sudden accumulation of wealth caused grave concern among his colleagues. A man of excessive tastes, Danton himself seems to have realized that he could not survive for long in the new atmosphere of moral virtue which the prim Robespierre was bringing to the revolution.

After the institution of the Terror, Danton seems to have lost his political enthusiasm, preferring to devote his energy to his new young wife (a fact which could only serve to confirm the Terrorists' low opinion of his moral character.) Undeniably one of the ablest of the revolutionary politicians, Danton's real motivation and allegiance remain uncertain. The champion of the people or a shrewd self-interested opportunist? – More than any other figure of the period, Danton remains a source of fierce controversy among historians and one of the enigmas of the Revolution.

Chapter Six

THE TERROR

THE GREAT COMMITTEE OF PUBLIC SAFETY OF THE YEAR II

The National Convention had been elected as an interim government, pending the creation of a Constitution based on universal suffrage. That Constitution was now ready, but the ascendant Montagnards were, not unnaturally, unwilling to relinquish power at such a critical stage of the revolution. In order to consolidate its position, and to resolve the problem of its unconstitutional nature, the Committee of Public Safety persuaded a frightened Convention to give it a vote of confidence, while the Constitution itself was placed, quite literally, under glass – being displayed in a cabinet at the Convention as though it were already some sort of sacred but

HÉRAULT DE SÉCHELLES
(EX 5 APRIL 1794)

ST-JUST

PRIEUR DE LA CÔTE D'OR

CARNOT

BILLAUD-VARENNE COLLOT D'HERBOIS

Louis Antoine de Saint-Just 1768-94
Considered by many to be the real driving force behind the Terror, this precocious young man (still only 24 at the start of the Revolution) was constantly at Robespierre's side urging him on should conscience ever cause him to hesitate in his appliction of swift and impersonal justice.
Maximilien Robespierre 1758-94 – Small, obsessively neat and looking like a leftover from the old regime rather than a committed revolutionary. Robespierre was now the most powerful member of the new government. His quiet and sombre character was more than compensated for by the passionate sincerity of his convictions.

irrelevant relic. On October 10th, at the instigation of St. Just, the Convention officially proclaimed the govenment as 'revolutionary until the peace'.

The Committee of Public Safety now ruled in France in the name of the Convention, and has rightly been described as the first effective executive government of the revolutionary period. The members of the Committee were all determined and intelligent men who were to display considerable ability in the exercise of their collective responsibilities. But it was the so called 'political wing' of Billaud – Varenne, Collot d'Herbois, Couthon and most importantly, Robespierre and St.Just, who were to occupy the centre of attention as they directed the application of the Terror. The Terror had been demanded by the Sans-Culottes, but it exceeded even their wildest dreams.

LINDET

ST-ANDRÉ

PRIEUR DE LA MARNE

BARÈRE

COUTHON

ROBESPIERRE

Devoted only to the Revolution, he was to display great strength of character in shouldering the responsibility for a dictatorship which he himself had long warned against. Apparently devoid of self-concern, Robespierre showed little interest in the social advantages which his position opened to him. During the Terror, while Robespierre was to all intents and purposes the master of France, he remained in his personal life no more than the humble lodger of the master-joiner Duplay and his family at their spartan residence on the Rue Saint-Honoré.

THE PHILOSOPHY OF THE TERROR

Terror would be a 'coercive power' of the revolutionary government. It would weed out the enemies of the Republic regardless of past loyalties and affections. Ruthless, remorseless and impersonal, it would be administered at the request and for the benefit of the nation.

> IF THE BASIS OF POPULAR GOVERNMENT IN TIME OF PEACE IS VIRTUE IN TIME OF REVOLUTION IT IS VIRTUE AND TERROR.

> VIRTUE! WITHOUT WHICH TERROR IS DISASTEROUS. AND TERROR WITHOUT WHICH VIRTUE IS POWERLESS.

TO MANY ROBESPIERRE WAS THE CONSCIENCE OF THE TERROR

> WE MAKE TOO MANY LAWS AND TOO FEW EXAMPLES ROBESPIERRE.

> YES ST JUST WE MUST IMPOSE THE ONE WILL THAT EVERYTHING MAY TEND TO THE GOOD.

...AND ST-JUST ITS SOUL.

For the remaining months of 1793, the full force of the Terror was directed against the most vocal of the Mountain's opponents. In a series of 'great trials', Royalists, Girondins and Feuillants were subjected to the ultimate censorship of the guillotine.

OH LIBERTY, WHAT CRIMES ARE COMMITTED IN YOUR NAME!

MARIE ANTOINETTE
EX 16 OCT 1793

MADAME ROLAND
EX 8 NOV 1793

BRISSOT
EX 31 OCT 1793

BARNAVE
EX NOV 1793

FABRE D'EGLANTINE

But with the opposition eliminated, the Terror sought new victims from among supporters of the Mountain itself. Men such as Fabre d'Eglantine, the young architect of the revolutionary calendar, soon to be accused of corruption and added to the growing list of victims.

THE MACHINERY OF THE TERROR

THE COMMITTEE OF PUBLIC SAFETY

The principle organ and brain of the Terror. Its unchanging membership was re-elected from month to month.

THE COMMITTEE OF GENERAL SECURITY

Responsible for control of the police and internal security. Its overall direction of the Terror was minimal, and was to find itself increasingly in open conflict with the Committee of Public Safety.

THE REVOLUTIONARY TRIBUNAL

Divided into 4 sections, these were the courts of the Terror, without jury and against whose verdict there was no appeal.

Beneath the two main committees were twelve executive commissions and a host of bureaus and agencies, all directly responsible to the Committee of Public Safety.

After Robespierre himself, there was probably no other functionary of the Terror as greatly feared as Antoine Fouquier-Tinville (1746-95). This pale, thin-lipped ex-lawyer had been appointed to the Revolutionary Tribunal in 1793, where his outspoken denunciation of his colleagues' 'indulgence' favourably impressed Robespierre and was instrumental in his appointment as Public Prosecutor. Widely regarded as incorruptible, he was nonetheless perfectly willing to cut through the formality of court procedure, justifying himself in private with the comment, "When Robespierre has pointed out anyone to me, there is no help for it." A realist, he carried out the dictates of the Committee of Public Safety whilst maintaining an outward show of legal respectability. Calm and precise by nature, Fouquier-Tinville was to approach his own trial in December 1794 with astonishing self-assurance, so much so that eyewitness accounts report him as being sound asleep during the reading of the charges.

DEPUTIES ON MISSION

These were the agents of the Central Committee. Delegated to supervise the recruitment of troops and the arrest of suspects, they were given considerable discretionary powers. While most Deputies found the problems of recruitment and food supply more than enough to contend with, a minority indulged their sadistic instincts in a series of provincial executions which made even the Parisian Terror seem tame by comparison. Several of the more notorious of these Deputies were considered by their contemporaries to be little short of insane.

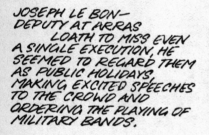

JOSEPH LE BON—
DEPUTY AT ARRAS
LOATH TO MISS EVEN A SINGLE EXECUTION, HE SEEMED TO REGARD THEM AS PUBLIC HOLIDAYS, MAKING EXCITED SPEECHES TO THE CROWD AND ORDERING THE PLAYING OF MILITARY BANDS.

JOSEPH FOUCHÉ – LYONS
IMPATIENT AT THE SLOW PROGRESS OF THE GUILLOTINE HE SPEEDED UP THE PROCESS BY ANNIHILATING HIS PRISONERS WITH CANNON FIRE.

JEAN BAPTISTE CARRIER—
DEPUTY AT NANTES
SOLVED THE PROBLEM OF A PRISON EPIDEMIC SPREAD BY OVERCROWDING BY HERDING SEVERAL THOUSAND SUSPECTS INTO BARGES WHICH WERE THEN SUNK IN THE LOIRE. THE RIVER RAPIDLY BECAME SO CONGESTED WITH THE BODIES OF THE DEAD THAT ALL FISHING WAS BANNED FOR FEAR OF CONTAMINATION.

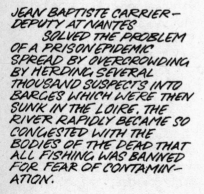

Alarmed by their inability to control the more extreme Deputies 'en mission', the Committee of Public Safety took steps to regain control of the provinces. The decree of 14 Frimaire, Year II (November 18 1793), placed all subordinate authorities and officials, except the police, under the direct authority of the Committee. The delegation of power, including that to the Deputies en mission, was banned. National agents were dispatched to the districts to implement the decrees of the central government, being required to report back to the Committee at ten day intervals.

The all-powerful Committee was now ready to dispose of its opponents within the Mountain.

The worsening economic situation had brought increasing criticism from the Hébertist faction, and in early 1794 their incitement of the Sans-Culottes led to an outbreak of strikes at the arms factories. While the Hébertists considered themselves to have the protection of Billaud-Varenne and Collot d'Herboise, they had reckoned without the determination of Robespierre who had lost all patience with them.

But to secure the elimination of The Hébertists, Robespierre was forced to sacrifice the 'Indulgents' – those convention members who were calling for moderation and an end to the Terror. While Robespierre himself had little love for these 'rotters' whom he regarded as agents of counter-revolution, they included in their ranks Danton and Desmoulins, both of whom he would have preferred to spare. Under pressure from Billaud-Varenne and Collot d'Herbois however, he had no choice but to affirm the impersonal nature of the Terror by agreeing to the destruction of his one-time friends.

THE DISINTEGRATION OF THE MOUNTAIN

The fall of 'Le Père Duchesne'

On 22nd Ventose, Year II (March 12, 1794) Hébert, together with several other Sans-Culotte Deputies, was arrested.

éloigné , foutre',
appellé roi, sortoit
sailles, soit   r ve
devant la chasse de
laquelle il ne croy
Verd, et pour faire
sujet de la naissa
il n'étoit que le p
une guerre sangla
laisirs de
raux,
e pau
plev
talon
su
v
pe
. s
so
y

Je suis le véritable Père Duchesne ; foutre !

LA PLUS GRAND
DE TOUTES LES J
DU
PERE DUCHESNE

APRES avoir vu, de ses propres yeux,
de véto fémelle séparée de son foutu
grue. Grand détail sur l'interroga
jugement de la louve autrichienne
grande colère contre les deux
diable qui ont osé plaider la ca

Accused of 'dishonesty' and complicity in a vague 'foreign plot', all were executed on 4th Germinal (March 24th).

The fall of Citizen Danton

Two days before the execution of Hébert, Danton and Robespierre attended a dinner party. It was to be their final meeting and, as their reported conversation shows, their final argument.

Within a week, Danton was arrested along with the other 'Indulgents'. Denied the opportunity to speak in their own defence, Danton, Desmoulins and 18 others were implicated in the overworked 'foreign plot' and executed on 16th Germinal (April 5th).

THE CULT OF THE SUPREME BEING

The year II saw the government embark on a formal policy of dechristianization. With the majority of the clergy, constitutional or otherwise, fiercely critical of the Mountain, the new regime found it wise to encourage the growth of a revolutionary cult based on liberty and reason. The introduction of the Republican calendar, the transformation of Notre Dame into the Temple of Reason, the erection of signs outside cemeteries announcing that 'Death is an eternal sleep', and the eventual closure of the Paris churches, were aspects of the violent anti-Christian sentiment which swept the country.

But dechristianization itself posed a major problem to the government. To Robespierre, it implied atheism and immorality which had no place in the new 'Republic of Virtue', and an enormous effort was made to channel anti-Christian feeling into an alternative religion which sought to explain the revolution in metaphysical terms. This 'Cult of the Supreme Being' was finally adopted as the new state religion in the spring of 1794.

The adoption of the new Revolutionary calendar in the autumn of 1793 marked a complete break with the old Christian era. Dating from the first day of the Republic (September 22nd, 1792), the new system renamed each month according to the seasons and replaced all reference to religious feasts and ceremonies with a purely secular terminology relating to tools or everyday objects.

(A more detailed explanation of the new calendar can be found amongst the appendices of the book.)

THE FESTIVAL OF THE
SUPREME BEING
8 JUNE 1794 (20 PRAIRIAL)

NATURE IS THE PRIEST OF THE SUPREME BEING; HIS TEMPLE IS THE UNIVERSE; HIS WORSHIP IS VIRTUE; HIS FEASTS ARE THE HAPPINESS OF A GREAT PEOPLE ASSEMBLED UNDER HIS EYS TO RENEW PLEASANT TIES OF UNIVERSAL BROTHERHOOD AND TO PRESENT THE HOMAGE OF SENSITIVE AND PURE HEARTS.

To the traditional enemies of the Revolution, royalists, rebels, speculators and food-hoarders, the Terror added a whole new category of offenders – 'The Incivisme' prostitutes, atheists, dissenters, the immoral or the merely indifferent – all were condemned as enemies of 'Virtue'.

With the simple fact of being 'denounced' (whether for good reasons or through personal spite) becoming virtually enough in itself to warrant execution, the common people of France found themselves threatened just as much as any aristocrat or dissenting politician. The total number of those tried and executed during the Terror has been estimated at around 17,000 (2,500 in Paris alone); while the addition of executions without trial, prison mortalities etc. could yield a final total of between 35 to 40,000 dead. Of these only 15% were clergy and nobility, while a massive 85% consisted of bourgeoisie, peasantry and workers.

"I know but two parties, that of good citizens and that of the bad. Patriotism is not a party matter, but a matter of the heart."

Robespierre

THE ARMY OF THE YEAR II

The setbacks of 1793 showed that the army was badly in need of reorganization if it was to constitute an effective fighting force. To the regular army, the National Guard and the numerous enthusiastic but poorly trained volunteer units, the levy 'en masse' now added a further 3/4 million raw conscripts. What, if anything, could be done with such a motley collection of troops?

The military authorities decided to merge the regulars and the volunteer units together under the command of professional offcers. The egalitarian practice of electing officers, common among the volunteers, was discarded and the infantry became organized into 213 Demi-Brigades consisting of 1/3 regular troops to 2/3 conscripts or volunteers. The blue uniform of the National Guard now completely replaced the old royalist whites.

The armies of Prussia and Austria consisted largely of mercenaries and conscripts lacking the revolutionary fervour of the French. They fought in long rigid lines, firing by volley with mechanical precision. The French, unable to cope with sophisticated military drill, formed into dense masses, which, when in motion, more than made up for their lack of firepower by the irresistible momentum of their advance. In this way the French conscripts, backed by well-equipped artillery, were able to achieve considerable success over their enemies.

By 1794 the French army had proved itself the master of the battle field. The one thing it still lacked was a general capable of harnessing such a force to win not just isolated battles but a complete campaign.

The threat of invasion was dispelled by a decisive victory over the Austrians at Wattignies (October 16th, 1793) and the following day the Vendéans were defeated at Cholet. With Toulon retaken from the British (December 19th), the Republic was safe. In the spring of 1794 the French took the offensive, defeating the Austrians at Tourcoing (May 18th) and Fleurus (June 26th) and recapturing Belgium.

AH JUST IN TIME THE SOUP WAS GETTING A BIT THIN.

SOUP OF VICTORY

FLEURUS

WATTIGNIES

MUCH OF THE CREDIT FOR THE FRENCH RECOVERY WAS DUE TO LAZARE NICHOLAS CARNOT (1753-1823). A FORMER MILITARY ENGINEER, HIS RESTRUCTURING OF THE FRENCH FORCES TOGETHER WITH HIS PERSONAL LEADERSHIP AT WATTIGNIES EARNED HIM THE EPITHET OF 'ORGANIZER OF VICTORY' - A TITLE WHICH HE WAS TO BE THANKFULL FOR IN THE FUTURE.

PLAN FOR FORTRESS

As the Coalition forces falter, France takes the offensive

BRITISH/DUTCH

Dunkirk

Hondschoote
8 Sept 93

Brussels

AUSTRIANS

Cologne

Neerwinden
18 March 93

Fleurus
26 June 94

Lille

Wattignies
16 Oct 93

PRUSSIANS

Amiens

JOURDAN/CARNOT

Meuse

Verdun

NORMANDY

Seine

Paris

Marne

HOCHE

PICHEGRU

Strasbourg

BRITTANY

Moselle

ROYALISTS

Loire

Tours

Nantes

LA VENDÉE

Lyons

SARDINIANS

Bordeaux

Bayonne

Toulouse

Toulon

SPANISH

SPANISH

BRITISH/ROYALISTS

Rhine

areas in revolt

Coalition offensives 1793

French counter-offensives
1793/4

French offensives 1794

Battles (French victories in bold)

Pursuing their impersonal policy of Terror, the Committee of Public Safety became increasingly alienated from both the popular movement and the wealthy bourgeoisie. Under the terrorist dictatorship, the independence of the press had all but disappeared, while the majority of political clubs had fearfully slid into self-imposed oblivion. The Jacobin clubs, admittedly, still flourished – but with a membership largely consisting of direct functionaries of the Terror. The controlled economy was subjugated almost entirely to the needs of the war; and while the Sans-Culottes resented the lack of importance attached to questions of social reform, the bourgeoisie were equally aggrieved by price controls, which inevitably ate into their profits.

The law of 22nd Pairial (June 10th, 1794) considerably simplified the application of the Terror by speeding up court procedure, refusing suspects the right of counsel and allowing only one of two verdicts – complete aquittal or death. With prisoners tried in large 'batches', the number of convictions rose steeply over the next month, causing considerable alarm among the members of the Convention. The Plain, especially, thought that with the danger of invasion receding the Terror could no longer be justified and should be stopped. To the Plain, Robespierre was the Terror. How to attack him without exposing themselves to the retributive blade of the guillotine? The solution to their dilemma was to come from an unexpected source – Robespierre himself.

Exasperated by continual bickering within the Committee of Public Safety, Robespierre's normal self-control seems to have deserted him during the month of Messidor (June 19 – July 18), and for the whole of this period he was absent from the meetings of the Committee, refusing any attempts at reconciliation. Isolated from all but the loyal St. Just and Couthon, he nevertheless entered the Convention on 8th Thermidor (July 26th) to launch an impassioned call for unity of government and to denounce his critics as enemies of the state. Called upon to specify the names of those so accused, Robespierre deferred the reading of his 'list', claiming that the time was 'not yet ripe'. This premature announcement of his intentions was a fatal mistake, for while it made each member acutely aware that his name might be included on Robespierre's list, it also gave the Convention time in which to gather its courage for a pre-emptive attack on the would-be accuser.

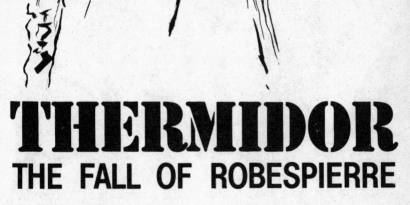

THERMIDOR
THE FALL OF ROBESPIERRE

On the following day, as Robespierre and St. Just prepared to read out the infamous list, they were both prevented from speaking, denounced as tyrants and arrested together with Couthon, Robespierre's brother Augustin and, at his own insistence, the Duplay's son-in-law, Phillip Le Bas. The prisoners were quickly dispatched to separate prisons as the Convention anxiously awaited the reaction of the Jacobins of the Paris Commune.

HIS JAW SHATTERED, ROBESPIERRE IS DRAGGED FROM THE HÔTEL DE VILLE

DECLARATION DES DROITS
DE L'HOMME ET DE CITOYEN

Declaring itself to be in a state of insurrection, the Commune released the prisoners and took them to the safety of the Hôtel de Ville. National Guardsmen under the command of Hanriot surrounded the Convention, and for a moment it appeared that the deputies had succeeded only in bringing about their own destruction. Hanriot, however, proved an incompetent leader, and after several hours standing in the rain waiting for orders which never materialized, the apathy of the Guardsmen prevailed with most of them drifting back to their homes.

THE DAYS OF THE TERROR ARE OVER!

MARAT

By one in the morning, the threat to the Convention had completely evaporated. Guards from those sections which had declared for the Convention were led to the Hôtel de Ville to rearrest the prisoners. Amidst scenes of incredible confusion, Le Bas committed suicide, while Robespierre was shot through the jaw (whether by his own hand or that of another remains unclear). Later that afternoon, the two Robespierres, St. Just, Couthon and 18 members of the Commune were delivered to the Place de la Revolution for execution. At around 8 in the evening, the wounded Robespierre was carried to the guillotine. The man once proclaimed the saviour was now condemned as the monster of the Revolution.

The end of the popular Revolution

In the final analysis, the Terrorist regime fell because the Sans-Culottes allowed it to fall. The reason for this lies largely in the Terror's own thoroughness. Called into existence to protect the Republic from a real or imagined aristocratic reaction, the Terror ensured the success of the Revolution by eliminating anyone who could be considered a threat. But as fear of the aristos faded so too did the revolutionary zeal of the people. The eradication of the Hébertists removed exactly those leaders most capable of reinspiring them. Under Robespierre's direction, the Terror became increasingly impersonal – a perfect instrument of 'Virtue'. To rouse themselves in the defence of such an abstract ideal, the Sans-Culottes needed something more than a Hanriot. (Executed along with Robespierre, Hanriot died as he had lived – in a druken stupor.) The Sans-Culottes had demanded terror, but effective terror inevitably curtailed the freedom of the popular movement, arresting its growth by inhibiting its principal organs: the journals and popular societies. When reaction came it found the crucial link between politicians and Sans-Culottes stretched so thinly that a drop of rain was able to destroy it. In 1789, the nascent popular movement had saved the Bourgeois Revolution. In 1792, it had transformed it. But the 'men of August' were gone, the Bourgeois Revolution was back in town . . . and the experiment in 'social democracy' was over.

MERDE !

Chapter Seven

The Thermidorian Reaction

M. J. Maximilien ROBESPIERRE,
surnommé le Catilina moderne,
e·é n·é le 10 Thermidor en 2e. de la république.
Lat.

J'ai joué les Français et la divinité....
Je meurs sur l'échaufaud je l'ai bien mérité

The men of Thermidor

With the powers of the Committee of Public Safety diminished and a new law decreeing the replacement of one quarter of each Committee with new members every month, the surviving Terrorists soon lost their positions of influence. They were replaced by Thermidorians drawn largely from the Plain or from among those more moderate Montagnards who had long been critical of their own party's policies.

Compared to their predecessors, the Thermidorians were as anonymous as their politics, which were essentially defensive and conservative. A party of the centre, they stood between the remains of the Jacobins on the left and a newly reawakening Monarchist party on the right. By playing off these groups against each other, the Thermidorians were able to maintain their own control of the government.

PAUL BARRAS

JEAN JACQUES REGIS DE CAMBACÉRÈS

LOUIS-STANISLAS FÉRON

JEAN-LAMBERT TALLIEN

Representing those upper bourgeois who had benefitted most from the revolution, the Thermidorians also found the army sympathetic to their ideals. This new alliance was to become increasingly significant with the passage of time.

'PARIS DANSE'

Thermidor also saw the re-emergence of Parisian society. Theatres reopened and new salons were established, the most popular being that of Madame Tallien – 'Our Lady of Thermidor'.

THE WHITE TERROR

AS REACTION INCREASES AND THE RIGHT ASSUME CONTROL OF THE PARIS SECTIONS GANGS OF ARMED YOUTHS KNOWN AS THE JEUNESSE DORÉES OR 'MUSCADINS' BEGIN TO TAKE THE LAW INTO THEIR OWN HANDS.

SOD OFF! MUSCADIN CREEPS

IN PARIS, STREET FIGHTS BREAK OUT BETWEEN MUSCADINS AND SANS-CULOTTES.

WHILE IN THE SOUTH JACOBIN SYMPATHISERS ARE MASSACRED BY THE FANATICAL 'COMPANIES OF JESUS'.

REPUBLICAN CLUBS ARE ATTACKED, BUSTS OF MORAT SMASHED AND HIS REMAINS REMOVED FROM THEIR PLACE OF HONOUR IN THE PANTHEON.

DESTROY THE RAT HOLES OF THE DRINKERS OF BLOOD.

SOCIETE DES JACOBINS UNITE, LIBERTE, EGALITE, INDIVISIBILITE DE LA REPUBLIQUE, FRATERNITE OU LA MO...

ANXIOUS TO APPEASE THE RIGHT THE GOVERNMENT SETS OUT TO DEAL WITH THE SURVIVING TERRORISTS, DEPORTING SEVERAL WITHOUT TRIAL TO THE 'DRY GUILLOTINE' OF GIANA. CONSIDERED INDISPENSABLE TO THE WAR EFFORT, CARNOT IS SPARED BUT FOUQUIER TINVILLE IS SENT TO TRIAL, AND SENTENCED TO THE FATE WHICH HE HIMSELF HAD INFLICTED ON SO MANY.

CARNOT COMITTEE OF —SPARED PUBLIC SAFETY

EXECUTED — FOUQUIER-TINVILLE PUBLIC PROSECUTOR

COLLOT D'HERBOIS COMITTEE OF PUBLIC SAFETY

BOTH EXILED TO GIANA

BILLAUD VARRENNE COMITTEE OF PUBLIC SAFETY

VADIER MEMBER OF COMITTEE OF GENERAL SECURITY

BARÈRE COMITTEE OF PUBLIC SAFETY SENTENCED TO EXILE BOTH ESCAPE INTO HIDING

135

Germinal

CHIEN PERDU
40 FRANCS

The hasty dismantling of the controlled economy and the resultant increase in the activity of speculators combined to make the winter of 1794/5 one of extreme hardship for the Parisian poor. Food prices and inflation reached unprecedented heights. Fearing hunger more than repression, the Sans-Culottes planned a mass expression of public indignation for the spring. The demonstration of 12th Germinal, Year III (April 1st, 1795) proved however to be a dismal failure. Lacking effective leadership, the unarmed protesters were easily dispersed by Guardsmen from the more prosperous districts; while those demonstrators who succeeded in invading the Convention were driven out by Muscadins armed with whips and cudgels.

Prairial

On 1st Prairial (May 20th) the Sans-Culottes attempted once again to regain the initiative. A far more threatening crowd of armed demonstrators converged on the Convention to demand the re-establishment of the Paris Commune. In the ensuing scuffle, the deputy Féraud was murdered and his head presented to the President of the Assembly. With some difficulty, the demonstrators were eventually ejected and the Convention determined to follow up their success by breaking the popular movement once and for all. For the first time since 1789, army troops were called into the city where they surrounded the Faubourg St-Antoine and starved its inhabitants into submission. Prairial was to be the last major attempt by the Sans-Culottes to influence the course of the Revolution – a Revolution now well beyond the reach of popular radicals.

Following the Germinal Prairial demonstrations, the White Terror was intensified. Active Sans-Culottes were rounded up and Jacobins forced from office. With opposition from the left a dead letter, the government was able to relax and concentrate its attention on the war.

DECEMBER – HOLLAND INVADED

JAN 22ND – THE DUTCH FLEET CAPTURED AT THE HELDER.

MAY 16TH – HOLLAND SURRENDERS.

JULY 22ND – SPAIN CONCLUDES PEACE WITH FRANCE.

APRIL 5TH – THE TREATY OF BASEL BRINGS PEACE WITH PRUSSIA.

Both internally and externally, the government now seemed secure. But if the left had been removed as an effective threat, the dormant royalist faction was about to pose new problems.

THE ROYALIST REVIVAL

On June 8th, 1795, Louis XVI's young son, regarded by royalists as Louis XVII, died in prison. In exile at Verona, the Comte de Provence immediately assumed the title of Louis XVIII. On the 24th he issued a manifesto promising a restoration of the old order and the punishment of the revolutionaries.

Given this new focus for their activities, royalist agitation increased. An emigré force landed by the British at Quiberon Bay (June 27th) was overwhelmingly crushed; but the Convention remained alarmed at the rapid growth of royalist feeling.

In the autumn of 1795 a new constitution was ready to be passed into law. Ironically, the constitution was intended to be ratified by a plebiscite based on universal suffrage. Ironic, because the constitution itself marked the abandonment of democratic principles and a return to indirect elections based on property qualifications.

Fearing the election of a large royalist bloc the convention proposed an amendment to the constitution calling for two thirds of the new assembly to be chosen from among the members of the Convention. The acceptance of the constitution and the law of the two-thirds (accepted by plebiscite – September 6th) brought fierce opposition from royalist sympathisers and forced the Thermidorians to look for support from the left. The disarmament of 'patriotic' Sans-Culottes was stopped and left-wing suspects were released from prison in anticipation of a royalist uprising.

The fears of the Thermidorians were justified when on the 12th Vendemaire, Year IV (October 5th, 1795) royalists in Paris rose in rebellion, established an insurrectionary committee and marched against the Tuileries. The uprising was easily crushed by troops under the command of Barras, but the events of Vendemaire brought to the fore a young officer of artillery whose decisiveness played a major part in the defeat of the rebels – His name was Napoleon Bonaparte....

139

While Vendemaire had removed any real threat of a royalist takeover, their deputies still constituted a force to be reckoned with in the newly elected legislative body which replaced the Convention in October 1795. Caught between the royalists (who had done well in the one-third of seats open to new members) and a large number of non-aligned deputies, the Thermidorians were still unquestionably the strongest group but did not constitute an outright majority.

On October 31st, however, the new assembly elected its executive government, the five man 'Directory'. The royalists could hardly expect any favours from the Directors – all were regicides who had voted for the death of Louis XVI.

Paul-François Barras 1755-1829 – An ex-Terrorist whose excesses as a 'Deputie en Mission' had brought him into conflict with Robespierre, Barras' command of the Convention's forces during the events of Thermidor had made him one of the most influential members of the new order. Dissolute and unprincipled, Barras' inclusion amongst the new directors was symptomatic of the degeneration of the revolutionary leadership into a self-obsessed bourgeoise clique unconcerned with the needs of a populace which had played no part in their election.

As if to emphasise the gulf between government and people, the Directors were issued with a uniform designed to display the importance of their position. For the modern observer, contemporary engravings of the Directors in their ludicrously over-elaborate costumes tend to suggest a pack of performing monkeys. Monkeys, however, who now held the fate of the Revolution in their hands.

Chapter Eight

THE DIRECTORY

FRANCE IN 1796

GOVERNMENT

At first sight, the Directory appears the ultimate bourgeois government; but closer inspection shows an unstable construct, with the separation of powers counterbalanced by a concentration of authority within the executive.

THE EXECUTIVE DIRECTORY

Five members elected for five years replaced by one new member each year. Appointed ministers, generals, commissioners of local administration. They did not have the power to dissolve the assemblies.
The original Directors were Carnot, Barras, Reubell, Letourneur and La Revellière-Lépeaux, all of whom had voted for the King's death.

THE MINISTRIES

Interior, Foreign Affairs, War, Marine, Justice, Finances, Police.

THE TREASURY

Independent from the Directory

THE COUNCIL OF ANCIENTS

Consisted of two hundred deputies. They elected the Directors and rejected or approved legislative resolutions formed by the lower council.

THE COUNCIL OF FIVE HUNDREDS

Put forward ten nominations for each post of Director. They were responsible for drafting legislative resolutions.

THE CHURCH

Despite the fact that Virtue and the Supreme Being had largely disappeared along with the Terrorists, Catholicism was still suppressed and most churches remained closed.

THE ARMY

The enthusiastic recruits of the Year II were now disciplined professionals. Senior officers from royalist backgrounds had long since been replaced by new generals, such as Bonaparte, Moreau and Massena – all solidly bourgeois.

INDUSTRY

The war had seen the decline rather than the expansion of capitalism. Large factories were relatively few, large scale production rare, and peasant small-holdings and town artisans remained the mainstay of economic life.

Very much a pioneer of the coming industrial age, Christopher Philippe Oberkampf was to establish the printed textiles industry in France during the Revolution.

THE RICH . . . .

For the *nouveau riche* created by the Revolution, the days of the Directory were a fine time. After a year of grey Robespierrean 'Virtue', the wealthy were eager to indulge themselves in the new decadence. Restaurants and dance-halls flourished, while gambling clubs and the 'private rooms' of the theatres offered every conceivable form of vice. Fashion reached new heights of ostentation, culminating in the outlandish eccentricities of the Jeunesse Doré, 'Incroyables' and their female companions, the 'Merveilleuses'.

Among the more bizarre phenomena of both the Thermidor and Directory periods were the macabre 'bals des victimes', at which relatives of those who had been executed during the Terror wore their hair up, as if in readiness for the guillotine, while around their necks they displayed pencil-thin bands of blood-red silk.

. . . AND THE POOR

For the poor times were, as usual, hard. Admittedly, things were not quite as bad as during the winter of 1794/5, but there had been no radical improvement either. Moreover, the gains of the year II had been swept away with the Terrorist regime. Social Security and the new education system had both vanished under the Thermidorians, while the decree authorizing the scale of emigré lands in small plots was revoked. Anticipating an expansion in industrial output, the wealthy bourgeois had no inclination to deplete the potential labour market by continuing to countenance the creation of small independent producers.

Pg 165

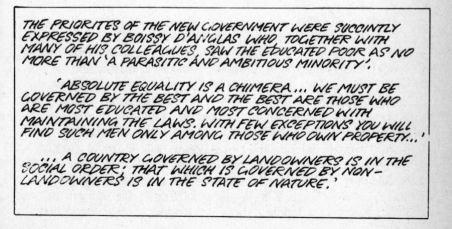

THE PRIORITES OF THE NEW GOVERNMENT WERE SUCCINTLY EXPRESSED BY BOISSY D'ANGLAS WHO, TOGETHER WITH MANY OF HIS COLLEAGUES, SAW THE EDUCATED POOR AS NO MORE THAN 'A PARASITIC AND AMBITIOUS MINORITY'.

'ABSOLUTE EQUALITY IS A CHIMERA ... WE MUST BE GOVERNED BY THE BEST AND THE BEST ARE THOSE WHO ARE MOST EDUCATED AND MOST CONCERNED WITH MAINTAINING THE LAWS. WITH FEW EXCEPTIONS YOU WILL FIND SUCH MEN ONLY AMONG THOSE WHO OWN PROPERTY...'

'... A COUNTRY GOVERNED BY LANDOWNERS IS IN THE SOCIAL ORDER; THAT WHICH IS GOVERNED BY NON-LANDOWNERS IS IN THE STATE OF NATURE.'

FRANCE IN 1796

France's financial and economic crises continued to worsen. By early 1796 the value of the assignat had dwindled to only 0.75% of its original value. With the notes so worthless even beggars refused to accept them, the assignats were finally discontinued in February.

Both militarily and economically, Britain remained France's main enemy. It was British gold which kept foreign armies in the field, while British naval supremacy had been largely responsible for the erosion of overseas trade. The French consoled themselves in the belief that 'Perfidious Albion' was merely a financial giant with feet of clay. In actual fact, the British exchequer had weathered its own financial crises extremely well, and British capitalism was developing at a prodigious rate – in complete contrast to the rest of Europe, especially France.

While peace could remove much of the strain on the French economy, the army remained committed to war. With the new generals become increasingly influential in French affairs, a solution had to be found which would be acceptable to both the Directory and the military commanders. The answer was simplicity itself; instead of stopping the war, France would extend its scope to areas hitherto largely untouched. The war of liberation was to be transformed into a war of conquest, with each newly acquired territory being ruthlessly exploited in order to help the home economy. With Belgium already absorbed into France, and Holland (now the Batavian Republic) a satellite state, the French offensive was now directed across the Rhine in the direction of Vienna. Napoleon Bonaparte prepared to deliver a secondary attack on the Italian kingdoms of Piedmont and Lombardy.

The first "total" war? — France's blueprint for military and economic victory.

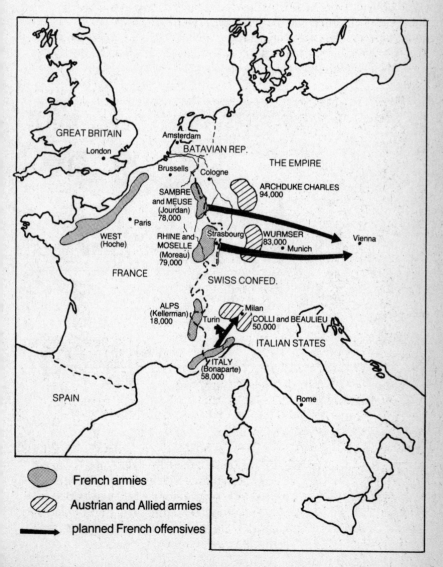

French armies

Austrian and Allied armies

planned French offensives

Who was Citizen ´Gracchus`?

The revolution is not yet complete because all the good things of life are taken by the rich who rule as dictators, while the poor toil in misery like slaves and are considered of no account by the state.

François Noël Babeuf.

On May 27th 1797, François Noël 'Gracchus' Babeuf, leader of the so called 'Conspiracy of Equals', was executed. Babeuf's primitive communism, based on distribution rather than production, and his badly managed plot to overthrow the government, are of little significance to the history of the revolution. But largely due to the efforts of his friend Buonarotti, his ideas were to have a considerable influence on Socialists and radicals of the 19th century. The following account of Babeuf's arrest is based on the report by Police Inspector Dossonville.

"I RECIEVED DIRECTIONS TO PUT INTO EXECUTION AN ORDER OF THE EXECUTIVE DIRECTORY AUTHORIZING THE ARREST OF BABEUF."

MERCERIE & SOIERIES
BERTIN

"President of the Republic, Citizen Carnot, had drawn up a plan of the locality where the insolent conspirator Babeuf was coolly calculating the overthrow of the constitution, organizing assassination and pillage, and meditating the ruin of the country"

YOU TWO STAND AT THAT END OF THE RUE VERDERET— LET NO ONE PASS.

"Being near the Halles (Markets) which might attract a crowd, I thought it wise to spread the report that a gang of thieves were to be arrested".

IT IS ALL OVER!— TYRANNY IS TOO MUCH FOR US.

"I entered the house and was upon them before they had so much as seen me".

WHY DO YOU OBEY MASTERS?

I OBEY A GOVERNMENT WHICH THE PEOPLE HAVE FRANKLY AND FREELY PRONOUNCED!

"Without wasting more time on useless talk I collected such papers as appeared to me best fitted to confirm the truth of this vast and odious conspiracy".

BRAVO! THE SCOUNDRELS ARE CAUGHT.

THIEF! THIEF!

"Babeuf was surprised to find himself greeted with cries of thief. Perhaps murderer would have been more appropriate, for by what he had proposed thirty thousand heads would have fallen".

"Nature has given to every man the right to the enjoyment of an equal share in all property." Babeuf.

Bonaparte in Italy

Resources for the Italian campaign were slender, but Bonaparte's ability to mass his troops quickly, regardless of the odds, and strike against the enemies' weakest point, soon led to repeated military success and the eventual conquest of all northern and central Italy. The French government could only look on in astonishment as he then proceeded to deal with the conquered territories without reference to the Directors.

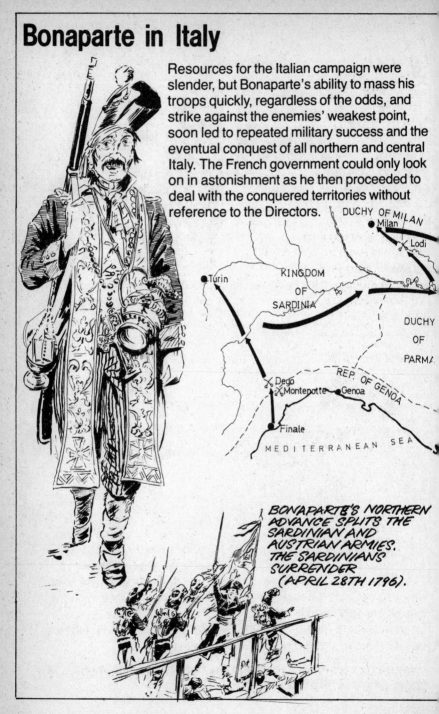

DUCHY OF MILAN
Milan
Lodi
Turin
KINGDOM OF SARDINIA
DUCHY OF PARMA
REP. OF GENOA
Dego
Montenotte
Genoa
Finale
MEDITERRANEAN SEA

BONAPARTE'S NORTHERN ADVANCE SPLITS THE SARDINIAN AND AUSTRIAN ARMIES. THE SARDINIANS SURRENDER (APRIL 28TH 1796).

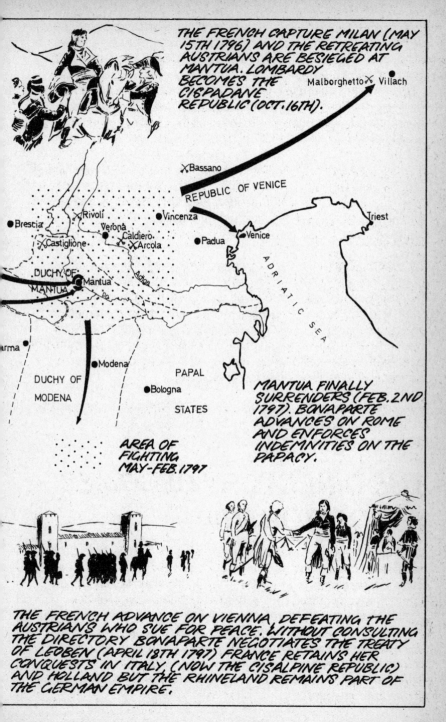

THE FRENCH CAPTURE MILAN (MAY 15TH 1796) AND THE RETREATING AUSTRIANS ARE BESIEGED AT MANTUA. LOMBARDY BECOMES THE CISPADANE REPUBLIC (OCT.16TH).

Malborghetto ✕ Villach

✕ Bassano

REPUBLIC OF VENICE

Brescia

Rivoli

Verona
Caldiero
✕ Castiglione
✕ Arcola

Vincenza

Triest

Padua

Venice

Adige

DUCHY OF MANTUA

Mantua

Po

ADRIATIC SEA

arma

Modena

DUCHY OF MODENA

Bologna

PAPAL

STATES

MANTUA FINALLY SURRENDERS (FEB.2ND 1797). BONAPARTE ADVANCES ON ROME AND ENFORCES INDEMNITIES ON THE PAPACY.

AREA OF FIGHTING MAY-FEB.1797

THE FRENCH ADVANCE ON VIENNA, DEFEATING THE AUSTRIANS WHO SUE FOR PEACE. WITHOUT CONSULTING THE DIRECTORY BONAPARTE NEGOTIATES THE TREATY OF LEOBEN (APRIL 18TH 1797) FRANCE RETAINS HER CONQUESTS IN ITALY (NOW THE CISALPINE REPUBLIC) AND HOLLAND BUT THE RHINELAND REMAINS PART OF THE GERMAN EMPIRE.

The Directory soon had more to worry about than Bonaparte. The elections of Germinal, Year V (April 1797) brought an unexpected swing to the right with pro-Royalists dominating the Council of 500. Aware that the President of the Council, Pichégru, was already in collusion with foreign powers, the Directors took alarm and summoned the troops to Paris. On 26th Messidor (July 14th) all right-wing sympathisers were ousted from the ministries and replaced by Republicans.

Royalist response was slow, and by the time the Council had finished debating its proposed indictment of the Directors, their opportunity had been lost. Instead, on 18th Fructidor (Sept. 4th), Pichégru and other leading pro-Royalists were arrested while the election of 177 council delegates was quashed. The Directory had become a dictatorship.

The elections of Floreal, Year VI (May 1798), again saw direct interference with the electoral process. Faced on this occasion with the prospect of a favourable result for the left, the Directory employed both bribery and intimidation to ensure the systematic disruption of polling. Despite the fact that the elections brought no great change in the make-up of the councils, the Directors determined to take no chances and on 22nd Floreal (May IIth) they barred 106 of the newly elected members from their seats.

Even the moderate Thermidorians of the councils were outraged by such high-handed behaviour and began to search for a way to rid themselves of the dictators.

THE DIRECTORY BECOMES A DICTATORSHIP

Favouring some form of compromise with the Councils, both Carnot and Barthelemy (replaced Letourneur May 1797) were proscribed following the events of Fructidor. Their successors, Merlin and de Neufchâteau (replaced by Treilhard after Floreal), were of little significance within the Directory, power being firmly concentrated in the new 'Triumvirate' of Barras, La Reveillière-Lepéaux and Reubell. Outspoken opponets of the new regime were either deported or tried by military courts and shot. This Terror, though shortlived and extremely limited in scope, contributed immensely to the unpopularity of the '2nd Directory'.

LA RÈVELLIÉRE-LÈPEAUX

REUBELL

BARRAS

The end of the First Coalition;

The treaty of Campo Formio (October 18th, 1797) had finally ratified the peace with Austria, but had inflicted far harsher terms than Bonaparte's Leoben treaty. With France obtaining the Rhineland along with her Italian conquests, it was inevitable that the Austrians would re-enter the war as soon as they had effected a recovery.

For the moment, the only country still at war with France was Britain. Despite stringent trade sanctions imposed on neutrals, the Directory

In early 1798 the seizure of Rome and the invasion of Switzerland had given France two new satellites from which she was able to derive a useful supply of funds through ruthless taxation.

Britain fights alone

was hard pressed to find an effective means of defeating this final enemy. For a while a direct invasion had seemed possible as French victories had put at her disposal a considerable fleet. The destruction of the Dutch fleet by the British admiral, Duncan (Camperdown, October 11th, 1797) and Jervis's successful blockade of a combined Franco-Spanish fleet at Cadiz, rendered the proposed invasion unfeasible and the idea was abandoned.

A small force was landed in Ireland to aid the Wolfe Tone rebellion of 1798. But its arrival came too late to help the rebels and the French forces were quickly surrounded and forced to surrender.

THEOBALD WOLFE TONE (1763-98) -LEADER OF THE UNSUCCESSFUL IRISH REBELLION OF '98. A PROTESTANT LAWYER FROM DUBLIN, HE WAS STRONGLY INFLUENCED BY THE JACOBINS IN FRANCE AND IS REGARDED AS THE FATHER OF IRISH REPUBLICANISM.

THE EGYPTIAN CAMPAIGN

Prompted by Bonaparte, the Directory had adopted a new plan to carry the war against the British – an invasion of the Levant which would poise the French for an attack on Britain's Eastern Empire.

In the spring of 1798, a vast fleet carrying a total of 38,000 troops sailed from Toulon. Capturing Malta en route (June 9th) the invasion force landed in Egypt, routed the Egyptian Mameluke army (July 21st) and entered Cairo. This initial promise was to be short-lived as on August 1st a British squadron under Nelson surprised and annihilated the French fleet at anchor in Aboukir Bay. Bonaparte and his army were trapped in Egypt. Bonaparte himself remained in Egypt for another year, constantly struggling to hold down a hostile population and engaging in an unsuccessful attempt to invade Syria (February 1799). Finally in August 1799, Bonaparte abandoned his troops and sailed for France, leaving the army to fight on alone for another two years.

Egyptology

While Bonaparte's campaign was doomed to failure, the invasion had at least opened Egypt to the outside world. Long since a source of curiosity to Western scientists and historians, the expedition was to bring in its wake a flood of scholars anxious to learn more about the ancient civilization of the Nile Valley. This research was to bear fruit in the eventual publication of a massive 24 volume *Description de l'Egypte* – the first reliable account of the monuments of Ancient Egypt, and the stimulus for the development of the science of Egyptology during the nineteeth-century. Many of the most important French discoveries (such as the famous Rosetta Stone – key to the translation of hieroglyphic inscriptions) were to fall into English hands after the destruction of the French Mediterranean Navy in 1799, and eventually find their way into the British Museum. It was probably also the English who started the unjustified but still widely believed rumour that French troops had used the sphinx for target practice, shooting off its nose in the process.

THE SECOND COALITION

French expansion into Central Europe and the Levant led to the formation of a new Allied coalition. Once again, Britain was to provide both direction and finance while Prussian neutrality was to be more than compensated for by the intervention of Russia under the half-crazed Paul I.

BRITAIN

SWEDE

TAXES

INDEMNIT

WAR BOOTY

FRANCE

RASTATT

URGED ON BY HIS WIFE, THE FRANCOPHOBE MARIA CAROLINA (SISTER OF MARIE ANTOINETTE), FERDINAND IV OF NAPLES INVADES THE ROMAN REPUBLIC — A DOOMED VENTURE WHICH LEADS TO THE SIEZURE OF NAPLES BY CHAMPIONNET, THE SELF STYLED 'BONAPARTE' OF SOUTHERN ITALY'.

The war quickly took on a sensational nature when French delegates to a conference at Rastatt were apparently asassinated by Austrian Hussars ('apparently' as the murderers were never traced). Despite her accumulation of war booty, the advent of hostilities found France unprepared. Understrength and short on supplies, the French army nevertheless attacked on all fronts, only to be beaten back by the numerically superior coalition forces.

PRUSSIA

RUSSIA

AUSTRIA

NAPLES

BONAPARTE IN EGYPT

CRISIS OF THE SUMMER OF 1799

In the wake of continuing military defeat, Reubell resigned from the Directory in the spring of 1799. Still smarting from the Floreal coup, the Councils seized the opportunity to have Sieyés, a known enemy of the Directors, elected as his replacement. Forming an immediate alliance with Barras, Sieyés was able to exert considerable pressure on the remaining Directors to step down. On June 16th, Trelhard was forced from office, while two days later on 30th Prairial, La Revellière-Lépaux and Merlin followed. They were replaced by Gohier, Ducos and significantly, Moulin – a Jacobin. With Jacobins also assuming positions of influence within the various ministries, the resurgence of the left seemed assured.

This impression was reinforced by the voting of a series of 'Jacobin Laws' which established in effect another levy 'en-masse', increased requisitioning and authorised the internment of relatives of emigrés and rebels in Departments declared to be in a state of disturbance. Agitation increased for the indictment of the former Directors, and on September 13th the pro-Jacobin General Jourdan called for the country to be declared 'in danger'.

To the Thermidorians of the Councils, the phrase 'in danger' implied emergency powers and the creation of a revolutionary government. Alarmed by the prospect of a new terror, they refused to give way to the Jacobins and under the leadership of Sieyés they were able to defeat the proposed indictments by 217 votes to 214. With the Sans-Culottes indifferent and disorganized after years of reaction, the Jacobins were unable to call on popular support, and the government remained in the control of moderates.

MASSENA

Massena's victory at Zurich (Sept. 27th) stopped the allied advance and momentarily dissipated the impetus of the Jacobin cause. Sieyés, however, remained aware that a future defeat could easily revive their demands. Searching for a more permanent solution, he received it in the landing of Bonaparte on October 9th and immediately began to formulate the coup which was to transform France into a military dictatorship.

THE BRUMAIRE COUP

It is ironic that Sièyes – the initial voice of the Revolution – should now become the instrument of its destruction. What were his motives as he carefully planned the coup which was to bring the Revolution to its close?

WHY A DICTATORSHIP?

"WHILE THE WAR CONTINUES ONLY A STRONG CENTRALIZED ADMINISTRATION CAN ENSURE THE PERMANENCE OF THOSE BENEFITS WHICH THE BOURGEOIS HAVE DERIVED FROM THE REVOLUTION."

WHY THE MILITARY?

"WE ARE STILL VULNERABLE TO PRESSURE FROM BOTH RIGHT AND LEFT. THE ARMY IS COMMITTED TO THE IDEALS OF THE BOURGEOIS REVOLUTION AND HAS THE STRENGTH TO SMASH ANY ROYALIST OR JACOBIN RESURGENCE"

WHY BONAPARTE?

"AS OUR MOST SUCCESSFUL GENERAL HE COMMANDS BOTH ADMIRATION AND RESPECT. MOREOVER, HIS UNEXPECTED ARRIVAL IN FRANCE MAKES HIM THE RIGHT MAN IN THE RIGHT PLACE AT THE RIGHT TIME!"

WHO ARE THE OTHER CONSPIRATORS?

"THEY INCLUDE MINISTER OF JUSTICE CAMBACÉRÈS, PRESIDENT OF THE ELDERS LEMERCIER AND PRESIDENT OF THE 500 LUCIEN BONAPARTE. TOGETHER WITH THE CO-OPERATION OF BARRAS, THIS GIVES THE COUP SUPPORT IN ALL KEY AREAS."

18th BRUMAIRE, YEAR VIII (November 9 1799)
Invoking a mythical terrorist conspiracy, Sièyes pursuades the Councils to move to St Cloud on the outskirts of Paris. Bonaparte is made commander of the Paris garrison. Barras resigns from office while Gohier and Moulin are held prisoner.

19th BRUMAIRE. The army surround the palace as Bonaparte enters and denounces the Councils. The coup falters as the 500, unwilling to vote themselves out of existence, threaten to outlaw their accuser. The situation is resolved by Lucien Bonaparte who convinces the troops that Councillers in the pay of England have attacked their general with daggers. The 500 are forcibly ejected, a small number of them returning that evening to join the Elders in voting for the adjournment of the Councils, the preparation of a new constitution and the replacement of the Directors with 3 'Consuls' – Sièyes, Ducos and Bonaparte. THE REVOLUTION IS AT AN END

FRANCE STANDS POISED ON THE THRESHOLD OF THE NAPOLEONIC ERA!

PROCLAMATION
DU GÉNÉRAL EN CHEF
BONAPARTE.

Le 19 Brumaire, onze

A mon retour à Paris, j'ai trouvé la division dans toutes les Autorités, et l'accord établi sur cette seule vérité, que la Constitution était à moitié détruite et ne pouvait sauver la liberté.

Tous les partis sont venus à moi, m'ont confié leurs desseins, dévoilé leurs secrets, et m'ont demandé mon appui : j'ai refusé d'être l'homme d'un parti.

Le Conseil des Anciens m'a appelé ; j'ai répondu à son .... concerté

par des hommes en qui la nation est accoutumée à voir des défenseurs de la liberté, de l'égalité, de la propriété : ce plan demandait un examen calme, libre, exempt de toute influence et de toute crainte. En conséquence, le Conseil des Anciens a résolu la translation du Co.. législatif à Saint-Cloud ; il m'a chargé de la dispo. de la force nécessaire à son indépendance. J'ai cru d à mes concitoyens, aux soldats périssant dans nos a à la gloire nationale acquise au prix de leur sang, d'.. le commandement.

Les Conseils se rassemblent à Saint-Cloud ; les républicaines garantissent la sûreté au dehors ; plusieurs assassins établissent la terreur au dedans ; du Conseil des Cinq-cents, armés de stylets et d'a font circuler tout autour d'eux des menaces de r Les plans qui devaient être développés, son la majorité désorganisée, les Orateurs les plu ....és, et l'inutilité de toute proposition s ...... et ma douleur au..

BONAPART.

APPENDICES

Although the revolutionary calendar was officially introduced in 1793, it dates from the first day of the Republic, i.e. 22nd September, 1792. The new system consisted of 12 months, each divided into 3 'decades' of 10 days, with the tenth day replacing Sunday as the traditional holiday (a move which proved unpopular with the working population). The 365 days of the year were made up by the addition of five 'Jours Sans-Culottides, at the end of each year which were designated as public holidays. A leap year added a sixth Sans-Culottide to the calendar. The months were named after the attributions of the season in which they fell.

VENDÉMIARE (Latin, vindemia — vintage)	SEPT 22 — OCT 21
BRUMAIRE (Brume — mist)	OCT 22 — NOV 20
FRIMAIRE (frimas — frost)	NOV 21 — DEC 20
NIVÔSE (Latin, nivosus — snowy)	DEC 21 — JAN 19
PLUVIÔSE (Latin, rainy)	JAN 20 — FEB 18
VENTÔSE (Latin, ventosus — windy)	FEB 19 — MAR 20
GERMINAL (Latin, germen — bud)	MAR 21 — APR 19
FLORÉAL (Latin, florens — flowery)	APR 20 — MAY 19
PRAIRIAL (pré — meadow)	MAY 20 — JUN 18
MESSIDOR (Latin, messis — harvest)	JUN 19 — JUL 18
THERMIDOR (Greek, therme — heat)	JUL 19 — AUG 17
FRUCTIDOR (Latin, fructus — Fruit)	AUG 18 — SEP 16
SANS-CULOTTIDES	SEP 17 — SEP 21

(In a leap year, subtract one day from conventional Gregorian calendar dates after IIth Ventôse to give corresponding revolutionary date, e.g. Messidor, year IV becomes June 18 — July 17, 1796.)

Women and the Revolution

The French Revolution saw no perceptible improvement in the postion of women, with small gains, such as divorce and education, being quickly lost. In an age when political activity by women was regarded as little more than a joke, only a handful of such individuals emerge with any clarity from the period.

Olympe de Gouges – An early activist, her 'Declaration of the Rights of Women' serverely criticised the Declaration of 1789 for its lack of attention to women's rights. Despite the revolutionary nature of this document, she was herself basically conservative and was to be executed in 1793 for her pro-royalist views.

Pauline Léon and **Claire Lacombe** – Founders of the Society of Revolutionary Women. From its inception in February 1793 to its suppression under the Terrorist regime, this society became closely identified with the radical Hébertist faction, its members adopting the dress of the Sans-Culottes and playing a significant part in the disruption of Girondist meetings during the tense period leading up to the Terror. Incarcerated during the Terror both retired from politics after their release, taking with them into anonymity the last vestiges of revolutionary feminism.

Manon Philipon, Madame Roland – Both through her salon and her weak and malleable husband, Madame Roland was able to play a leading role in the affairs of the Gironde. After the fall of the monarchy, with the Girondin leadership in panic, she showed herself to be one of the calmest and most able of the group. Active on behalf of her class rather than her sex, her political power remained dependent on the mouthpiece of her husband. After Roland's resignation and flight from Paris in 1793, she was no longer taken seriously by friend or enemy alike. Displaying great strength of character she chose to remain in the city, battling to be heard until the very moment of her execution.

THE WORKING WOMEN OF PARIS ALSO PLAYED A ROLE IN THE PROGRESS OF THE REVOLUTION. NUMEROUS PETITIONS, DEMONSTRATIONS AND RIOTS APPEAR TO HAVE BEEN INSTIGATED BY WOMEN AND WHILE THEY SEEM TO HAVE TAKEN LITTLE PART IN THE RUNNING OF THE SECTIONS THEY COULD BE QUICK TO DEFEND THEIR RIGHT OF ATTENDENCE AT THE ASSEMBLIES, AS THE FOLLOWING INCIDENT BASED ON A REPORT TO THE COMMISSAIRE DE POLICE SHOWS...

GENERAL ASSEMBLY OF THE SECTION DE MONTBLANC —MAY 29TH 1793

I AM STILL WAITING TO BE HEARD.

VERY WELL— THE ASSEMBLY WILL HEAR THE CITIZEN CAPTAIN.

FIELVAL! LET FIELVAL SPEAK.

CITIZENS, THIS OVERCROWDING IS INTOLERABLE —HOW CAN WE DELIBERATE UNDER SUCH CONDITIONS?

WE MUST RID OURSELVES OF THOSE AMONGST US WHO SERVE NO USEFUL PURPOSE.

IN SHORT, I PROPOSE THAT ALL FEMALE CITIZENS BE BANNED FROM FUTURE MEETINGS.

TO THE DISGUST OF THE WOMEN IN THE GALLERIES, THE MOTION WAS PASSED.

MONSTEROUS! THIS IS NO PATRIOT.

I HOPE HIS WIFE MAY RID HERSELF OF HIM AS EASILY.

LATER AS THE CAPTAIN LEAVES THE HALL.

AND SO CAPTAIN FIELVAL... LIKE ANY GOOD POLITICIAN WHEN FACED WITH THE CONSEQUENCES OF HIS ACTIONS...

ROGUE SCOUNDREL

HANG HIM

TO THE LANTERN WITH HIM!

FLED!

REVOLUTION IN THE CARIBBEAN

In 1789 much of the wealth and confidence of the bourgeoisie came from their control and exploitation of France's most important surviving colony, San Domingo. It is unlikely that any of them either expected or welcomed the effect which the Revolution was to have on this small Caribbean Island.

The fall of the old regime exposed the deep divisions among the French colonists, with the new colonial assemblies degenerating into total confusion as the slave managers, stewards and tradesmen vied for power with the previously dominant plantation owners. Totally dependent on the slave economy, neither side were anxious to apply the principles of the 'Rights of Man' to the non-French population. The resulting increase in the oppression of Blacks led to a series of revolts and the emergence of a powerful new leader of the slave population, Toussaint-L'Ouverture (later to become known as 'Black Napoleon').

With the European war of 1793 extending itself to Domingo, Toussaint and his 600 strong force of slaves became, in effect, part of the Spanish army and were instrumental in Spain's conquest of much of Northern Domingo. The rise of the radicals in France, however, and the National Assembly's belated abolition of slavery (Feb. 1794), saw Toussaint allied to the French, and the British and Spanish forces expelled from the North by his steadily growing army (now numbering around 5000 men). Toussaint's increasing influence was eventually recognized with his appointment as Governor of the colony in 1797.

But while the Revolution advanced in Domingo under its new Governor, it was already in its death throes in France. The conservatives of the Directory were increasingly at odds with Toussaint; and the eventual emergence of Bonaparte led to the attempt to re-exploit the colony by forcible reintroduction of the slave system. With the Island occupied by a French force in February 1802, Toussaint and his army put up strenuous resistance until his arrest and deportation to France in June. But while Toussaint himself died as a captive, the spirit of independence which he had exemplified remained alive, and a further revolt against the occupying forces finally drove the French from the Island in 1803. In December of that year, Domingo became the independent nation of Haiti.

ART AND SCIENCE

By the late 18th Century, reaction against the whimsical Rococo style popular in the courts of France and Southern Germany had firmly established Neo-Classical austerity as the dominant artistic movement of the period. With its emphasis on morality, neo-classicism both nurtured and complemented that Robespierrean ideal of Virtue which was to become so prevalent in France. The real spirit of the Revolution, however, was not to find its reflection in the world of art until the revolutionary period itself was over. Ironically, it was outside France that the first glimmerings of the more expressive and emotive style began to appear. In the work of Blake in England, Goya in Spain and the Romantic writings of the German author Goethe, the influence of the revolutionary vision can be clearly discerned.

Despite the Constituent Assembly's institution of a national 'Pantheon' in which to exhibit works depicting revolutionary heroes, political art of the period did not amount to very much. Most painters were content to depict the serenity of the neo-classical landscape rather than risk an excursion into the rapidly shifting arena of political opinion. Probably the best known artist of the period was Jacques-Louis David who, although a noted Jacobin, was able to retain his pre-eminent position throughout both the revolutionary and Napoleonic eras. David's 'Death of Marat' was one of the few major political paintings of the period and the only real masterpiece to emerge during the Revolution.

RIGHT; 'THE TENNIS COURT OATH' BY DAVID

DAVID

The bourgeois revolution brought new scope and initiatives to the field of science and technology; but the turmoil and uncertainties of the period disrupted the successful completion of any constructive work. Nevertheless, a few notable advances were either made, or at least, initiated during these years.

In Paris, the Jacobin, Joseph-Marie Jaquard commenced the work which would eventually produce the first automated loom in 1803. The mechanism employed on this loom is regarded as the original forerunner of the modern computer.

In Lyons, a competition set by the Directory encouraged Nicholas Appert to begin investigations into food preservation which led to the devising of the canning process by 1810.

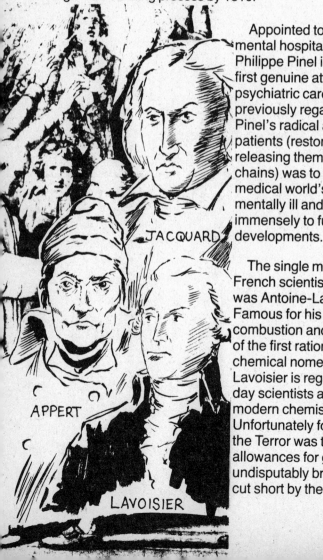

JACQUARD

APPERT

LAVOISIER

Appointed to the Bicêtre mental hospital in 1793, Dr Philippe Pinel introduced the first genuine attempts at psychiatric care of the insane previously regarded as criminal. Pinel's radical approach to his patients (restoring their dignity by releasing them from their chains) was to transform the medical world's view of the mentally ill and contribute immensely to future developments.

The single most outstanding French scientist of the period was Antoine-Laurent Lavoisier. Famous for his theory of combustion and the introduction of the first rational system of chemical nomenclature, Lavoisier is regarded by present day scientists as the father of modern chemistry. Unfortunately for Lavoisier, the Terror was to make no allowances for genius and his undisputably brilliant career was cut short by the guillotine in 1794.

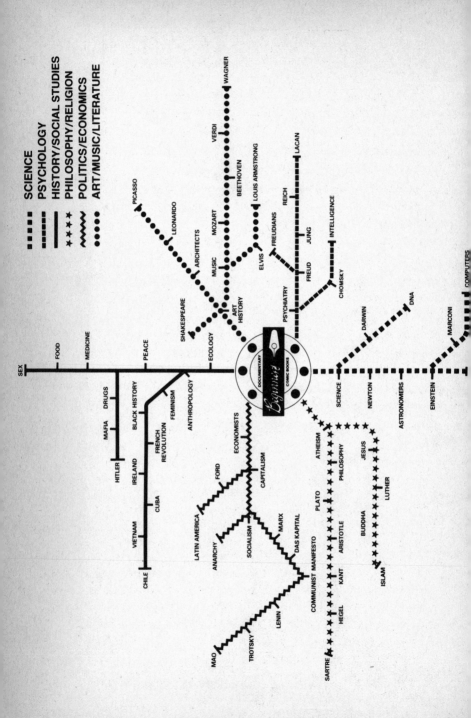